Building Tips
and Techniques

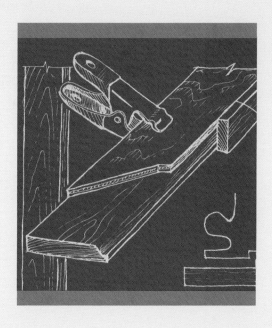

Edited and illustrated by Charles Miller

The Taunton Press
Inspiration for hands-on living®

The Taunton Press
Inspiration for hands-on living®

The Taunton Press, Inc., 63 South Main Street, PO Box 5506, Newtown, CT 06470-5506
e-mail: tp@taunton.com

Distributed by Publishers Group West

Editor: Charles Miller
Cover design: Cathy Cassidy
Interior design and layout: Mary McKeon
Illustrator: Charles Miller
Photographers: Mike Guertin, Randy O'Rourke

For Pros/By Pros® is a trademark of The Taunton Press, Inc., registered in the
U.S. Patent and Trademark Office.

Library of Congress Cataloging-in-Publication Data

Building tips and techniques / edited and illustrated by Charles Miller.
    p. cm. -- (Taunton's for pros by pros)
Includes bibliographical references and index.
 ISBN 1-56158-687-0
 1. Building--Miscellanea. I. Miller, Charles. II. For pros, by pros
TH7 .B84 2004
690'.837--dc22

                2003017441

Printed in the United States of America
10 9 8 7 6 5 4 3 2

This book is for my father, John Edwin Miller, who always told me,
"If you want to solve a problem, start by doing a drawing of it." Thanks, Dad.

—**Charles Miller**, *"Tips" editor*

Contents

Foreword

Over the entire history of *Fine Homebuilding* magazine, there have been two constants: a generous readership interested in sharing clever ideas and Chuck Miller, the editor and illustrator who brings those ideas to life in the "Tips & Techniques" department. From the first issue in 1981, the union of these constants has proved to be the most popular and useful part of the magazine. No surprise there.

Even on the best day, building or fixing houses is hard work. So any tip that helps you work better, faster, or less expensively is a valuable commodity. In fact, Chuck once remarked that tips are the "DNA of fine homebuilding," the fundamental genetic code upon which complex structures are built. But the tips themselves aren't necessarily complex. In fact, the best ones are what we call "forehead slappers." You're first response on seeing them is "Of course, why didn't I think of that?"

Many of our favorite tips come from professional tradesmen and represent the shortcuts and job-site solutions they've invented in their years of working on houses. Other tips come from amateur builders who didn't know how they were supposed to do something and, in figuring it out, came up with a better way. But whatever the source, all of the tips are good ideas. I know this to be true because I know the editor who evaluated them for publication.

Chuck Miller is *Fine Homebuilding*'s renaissance man, which is to say he's the only editor on the staff who can draw AND write. He's also a fine carpenter and an even better guitar player. All of which helps him produce the "Tips" department (don't ask how the guitar playing enters in). But Chuck doesn't just edit and illustrate the tips; he field-tests them, too. When someone thought it was a good idea to use upturned drywall buckets as stilts, Chuck screwed an old pair of sneakers to the bottoms of two buckets and clomped around a while. All part of the job.

Collected here are the best tips ever published in *Fine Homebuilding*, which means the best ideas, from the best builders, filtered though the best editor I know.

—*Kevin Ireton*, *editor-in-chief*, Fine Homebuilding

Note from the Editor

"My partner Jerry always reads the 'Tips & Techniques' column, and he won't even read stop signs."

That's probably the best compliment anybody ever paid this little bi-monthly tailgate session, where builders share their ingenious victories over job-site challenges. When I first came to work for *Fine Homebuilding* in 1980, I was lucky enough to be the guy that our art director wanted to edit and illustrate the "Tips & Techniques" column. As a remodeling contractor, I had already been doing similar drawings for the other guys on the crew. But most of those drawings were on scraps of drywall or plywood. Getting to work indoors, at a desk yet, is a real step up for a guy who's done his time in crawl spaces.

In addition to being a wellspring of useful advice, the "Tips" column plays a couple of other, less apparent roles. For many of our authors, "Tips" is the first place they get something published in our magazine. In fact, some of our all-time great editors launched their publishing careers here, by sending their favorite job-site solutions to the "Tips" column.

Evidence of the crafty nature of our tipsters can be found in the number of ideas that have been developed as commercially available products after first appearing in the "Tips" column. Examples of the tips that turned into products include adjustable flashlights, invisible drywall joints, soap pumps, stair-tread layout gauges, bucket stilts, and plastic pipe clamps, just to name a few.

But I think the best part about the "Tips" column is that it's a community of builders who genuinely get a kick out of sharing their ideas with others and have done so for a long time. More than once I've opened a tip from someone new that begins, "I've learned an awful lot from the 'Tips' column over the years, and I just wanted to repay the debt by sending in these ideas. Hope you can use them…"

One veteran tipster is Mike Guertin, and I'd like to thank him for selecting the 290-plus tips presented in this book from the hundreds that we've published in the last 23 years. Mike also built the projects and took the photos that help to illustrate this book.

When a tip needs a little tweaking, or some further explanation because I just don't get it, I turn to my trusty colleagues here at *Fine Homebuilding* for guidance—especially Kevin Ireton, Roe Osborn, and Andy Engel. Thanks, guys.

The largest debt of gratitude, however, goes to you tipsters out there who continue to amaze, delight, and educate us with your resourcefulness. Thank you for your contributions. Don't ever change, and don't forget to include your address.

—Charles Miller, "Tips" editor

1

Measuring, Marking & Layout

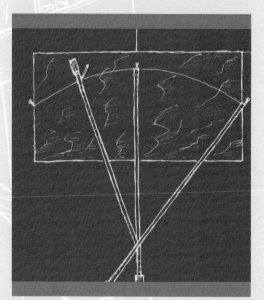

The Slip Stick

THIS VERSATILE TIME-SAVER uses a simple story-pole principle. I call it the slip stick, and I use it to measure distances between floor and ceiling without running up and down ladders or bending my tape into hard-to-read compound bends.

The basic components of the slip stick are an old tape, a few pieces of 1x stock and whatever hardware you have around to make it work. The first component is a 7-ft. U-shaped housing, as shown in the drawing at right. The second is a 6-ft. runner that fits inside the housing, where it can slide up or down. The runner has a portion of a tape-measure blade screwed to it. The portion of the tape you'll need is from the 7-ft. mark or so (attached to the top of the runner) down to about 13 ft. If you want to get fancy you can cut a concave curve into the runner, so the edges of the runner and tape will be flush.

Near the top of the assembly, I hold the two components together with a metal band that doubles as a reference point. It has to be precisely placed so that the tape at that point reads the exact length of the stick with the runner retracted. At the bottom of the runner I bolt a large washer on each face to keep the runner in the housing.

When my slip stick is closed, I can slip it under a ceiling of minimum height. With the 6-ft. runner extended, I can measure ceilings up to 13 ft. high. When I measure for a new wall in an old space, I cut the top and bottom plates and set one atop the other. With my slip stick on top of them, I can read the exact stud length without having to subtract the thickness of the plates.

—Sam Yoder, Cambridge, Mass.

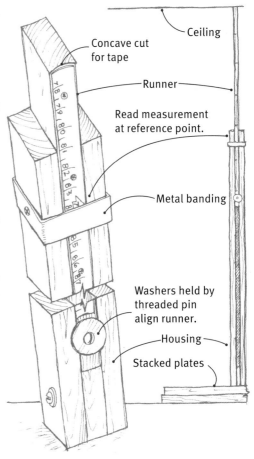

Ceiling

Concave cut for tape

Runner

Read measurement at reference point.

Metal banding

Washers held by threaded pin align runner.

Housing

Stacked plates

A Better Plumb Bob

I KEEP MY PLUMB-BOB STRING wound around a spool exactly 2 in. long. I drive a screw into one end of the spool, cut its head off, and grind the shank to a long, diamond-shaped point. Since I usually work by myself, I can drive the point into the top plate of the wall and dangle the plumb bob off the end of the spool. When the bob hangs 2 in. out from the bottom plate, I know the wall is plumb.

—Earl Roberts, Washington, D.C.

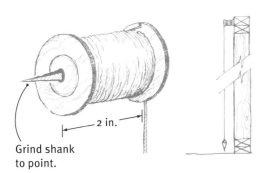

2 in.

Grind shank to point.

Stringline Anchor

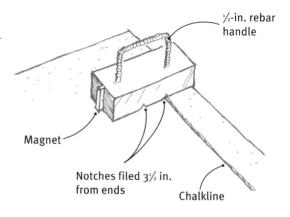

½-in. rebar handle

Magnet

Notches filed 3½ in. from ends

Chalkline

WHEN IT COMES TIME TO FRAME A HOUSE, I like to do the layout by myself. The solitude affords me time to work out the kinks in the plan without being barraged by questions from the crew. The problem is, it's tough to pop chalklines on a concrete slab (the typical foundation in my area) when you're working alone.

I solved the problem by getting a heavy piece of steel at a local scrapyard and welding a handle to it so I can lug it around more easily. This brick-size hunk of metal weighs about 20 lb., and it has no trouble anchoring the dumb end of a string line or steel tape. As shown in the drawing at right, I affixed a bar magnet to one end of the anchor to secure the hook on a steel tape. Also, I filed notches along the edges of the anchor, 3½ in. from the ends. When the end of the anchor is flush with the edge of the slab, either notch can be used to anchor my chalkline for a 2x4 layout.

Because of its mass and sharp angles, the anchor sometimes gets used as a job-site anvil. It is also useful for tying up the dog when necessary.

—Don Huebner, Austin, Tex.

Arch Layout

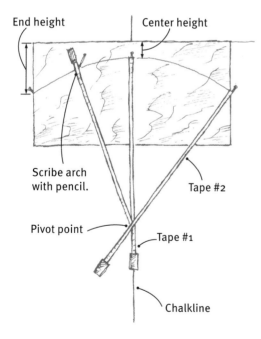

End height

Center height

Scribe arch with pencil.

Tape #2

Pivot point

Tape #1

Chalkline

HERE'S A WAY TO LAY OUT ARCHES that need to have specific heights at the ends or center, even though the spans vary. First, snap a long chalkline on the floor as shown in the drawing at left. Lay your material at one end, square to the line. After determining the span, end height, and center height, put the end of tape measure #1 at the center height and stretch it out next to the chalkline. Hook tape measure #2 on a nail located at the end height and stretch it out at an angle so that it intersects tape #1. Now move tape #2 until the numbers on both tapes match at the chalkline. Put a nail in the chalkline at this point. This is your pivot point. Hook one of your tapes over it and use it as a giant compass to trace your arch. On huge arches you can make one half and use it as a pattern.

—Spencer Thompson, Santa Monica, Calif.

Laying Out Winder Stairs

HERE'S AN EASY, ACCURATE WAY TO LAY OUT STAIRS that have wedge-shaped treads where the stair makes a 90° turn. This type of stair is called a winder, and it can bail you out of a situation where there isn't enough headroom for a standard landing.

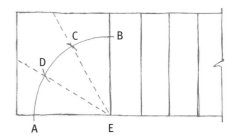

As shown in the drawing at right, use a compass to strike a radius from point E. The length of the radius isn't critical—it just needs to come down in the approximate point shown on the drawing. This arc determines points A and B. Now, using the same radius, swing an arc from point A to find point C, and from point B to find point D. Next, extend lines from point E through C and D to find the position of the risers for the treads.

By the way, local codes have different interpretations of how wide the treads need to be at a given distance from point E. Be sure to check with your inspector to find out what the requirements are.

—Kelly Johnston, Overland Park, Kans.

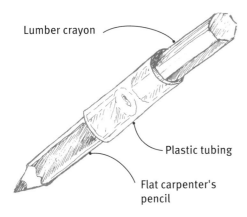

Lumber crayon

Plastic tubing

Flat carpenter's pencil

Framer's Layout Tool

THE WRITING INSTRUMENT SHOWN in the drawing at left eliminates fumbling around in your tool pouch for a pencil or a lumber crayon and always coming up with the wrong one. It also lets you get more use out of your lumber pencil because instead of tossing your pencil when it gets down below 2 in. long, the plastic tubing lets you use it right down to the nib.

—Todd Sauls, Carpinteria, Calif.

Durable Chalklines

CHALK LAYOUT LINES are invariably erased by brooms, rain, and shoes—especially on concrete. If you like to do your layout well in advance of the work it will guide, spray the lines with polyurethane varnish or some other clear finish. The lines will stay put until you need them.

—Dennis Lamonica, Panama, N.Y.

Adjustable Stair Jig

SOME CARPENTERS SWEAR BY STAIR GAUGES for use with a framing square during stair-stringer layout. But I've encountered problems with stair gauges. First, the cheaper six-sided gauges are difficult to set accurately because the edge of the gauge that contacts the edge of the lumber sits off the edge of the framing square. And while my good Starrett stair gauges align exactly with the edge of the square, they have not solved the problems posed by the lumber. The edges of lumber have defects: nicks, knotholes, and wane (sloped edges caused by the rounded edge of the tree). When the gauge falls on one of these imperfections, it throws off the layout.

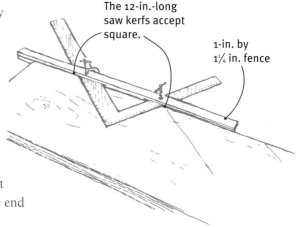

The 12-in.-long saw kerfs accept square.

1-in. by 1¼ in. fence

Another problem occurs when the lumber used for the stringer is just long enough for the layout. In these cases, for the first and/or last step, one of the gauges has nothing to bear against because it's off the end of the board.

Because of these problems, I've stopped using stair gauges to lay out stair stringers. Instead, I use a stair jig with an adjustable fence, as shown in the drawing at right. The jig consists of a framing square, a fence, and two tiny C-clamps. The fence is 32 in. long, a full 1 in. thick, and 1¼ in. wide.

To make the fence, I ripped a 12-in.-long kerf from each end of the fence, with the material standing on edge as I fed it into my tablesaw. I made this kerf in the center of the 1-in. thickness of the board. Stopping the rip at 12 in. left an area of uncut wood about 8 in. long in the center of the fence.

To set up the jig, I slide the fence over the legs of the rafter square, set it to the desired layout, and clamp it in place. In use, the fence rides along the board and easily bridges imperfections in the lumber. It also holds the square in the correct position right up to the end of the board. Once the fence is fabricated, it takes no longer to set up this jig than it does to affix stair gauges. This jig also can be used to lay out rafters.

—John Carroll, Raleigh, N.C.

Snapping Lines

WHEN SNAPPING A SERIES OF CHALK LINES, as on roofs or siding, two people can hook their chalk box lines at the clip by inserting one line through the other, as shown in the drawing at left. Worker A reels in the hooks to his end and they snap lines until worker B's line goes dry. Then worker B cranks his line while exposing A's for more snapping. There is no walking back and forth, and no time wasted rechalking the lines.

—Jackson Clark, Lawrence, Kans.

Lipstick on the Job

MORE THAN ONCE I'VE RECEIVED A LOOK OF DISBELIEF when I've asked a helper to get the lipstick from the truck. But the stuff comes in handy in a variety of situations.

When I need to mark the end of a door latch or deadbolt strike, I rub some lipstick on the bolt, close the door, and turn the bolt against the jamb to locate the proper spot to drill.

Drywall cutouts can be easily found by smearing the edges of the electrical box with the lipstick, hoisting the sheet of drywall into place, and pressing it against the outlet. Pull the drywall away from the box and make your cutout on the lipstick marks for a snug fit every time. This principle works for paneling and siding, too.

—Ernie Alé, Santa Ana Heights, Calif.

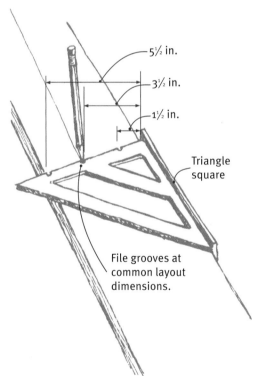

5½ in.

3½ in.

1½ in.

Triangle square

File grooves at common layout dimensions.

Triangle-Square Refinement

AS DO MANY OTHER CARPENTERS, I hope that the person who invented the triangle square ended up a rich man. In the past 20 years or so, these squares have become a standard in the trades because they are easy to use and convenient to carry. To make mine even more efficient, I filed grooves along the square leg to mark often-used dimensions. As shown in the drawing at left, I put grooves at 1½ in., 3½ in., and 5½ in. Putting a pencil in the appropriate groove and then sliding the square down a board makes for quick layout marks.

—Will Ruttencutter, Valdosta, Ga.

2

Horses, Benches, Boxes & Belts

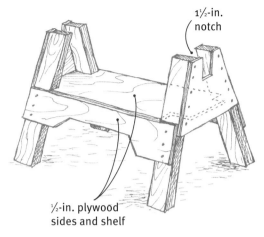

1½-in. notch

½-in. plywood sides and shelf

Another Sawhorse

I MADE THE SAWHORSE SHOWN IN THE DRAWING out of scraps, and I like it better than any I've used in the past. Its main feature is a 1½-in. notch at each end, which accepts a 2x crosspiece of any width. This allows me to replace this member easily when it gets abused. I can put in the exact height I need to match the level of a work table or bench. The notches also hold narrow pieces when I'm working on an edge. Two-by stock drops right in, and 1x material can be wedged tightly with shims.

To make the horse, I started with two ¾-in. plywood gussets on the ends screwed and glued to 2x4 legs. Then I let in a ½-in. plywood shelf notched around the legs. The shelf bears on the ½-in. plywood side pieces, which go on last. By making one horse a little longer than its brother, I can tuck the shorter one into it for easier transport.

—Sam Yoder, Cambridge, Mass.

Folding Horses

I CAN TRANSPORT MY WOODEN SAWHORSES in the trunk of my car and store them in tight spaces because I've designed them with folding legs. The trick is to build each leg pair as a unit with the cross-brace screwed in place. Attaching each leg unit to the horizontal member with a single carriage bolt lets the legs pivot. Ordinary hook-and-eye catches on each end will keep the horses steady while they are being used.

—Barry Bower, Baddeck, Nova Scotia

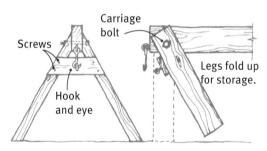

Carriage bolt

Screws

Hook and eye

Legs fold up for storage.

Belt-Buckle Upgrade

MY CARPENTER FRIENDS AND I HAVE ALL AGREED for some time that the weak link on a tool belt is the clasp. Some twist-grip buckles are flimsy, and they can all be clumsy to disengage, especially if you have to remove your belt in a precarious spot.

As a remedy, I removed my old clasp and replaced it with a seat-belt buckle. I tried both the push-button type and the spring type, and decided I like the spring type better. Now I can easily remove the belt when I want to, and with one hand, at that.

—Evan Disinger, Lemon Grove, Calif.

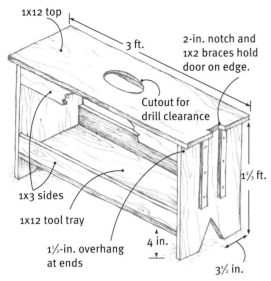

1x12 top

3 ft.

2-in. notch and
1x2 braces hold
door on edge.

Cutout for
drill clearance

1x3 sides

1x12 tool tray

1½-in. overhang
at ends

1⅔ ft.

4 in.

3½ in.

Lightweight Workbench

I GOT THE IDEA FOR THE WORKBENCH shown at left from a couple of old West Virginia carpenters. I've been using this design for years now, and the benches are unbeatable for holding work that's being drilled, cut, or nailed. Whenever I do drywall work, I lay two benches on their sides and cover them with planks and plywood to make a low scaffold. It's just the right height for working on an 8-ft. ceiling.

I've found these dimensions to be right for me, but of course they could easily be altered to suit the individual. The material for each bench costs less than $10. Nail them together with 8d cement-coated nails, and you're ready to work.

—Howard Goldblatt, McLean, Va.

Tool-Belt Tip

I USE SEPARATE POUCHES ON MY TOOL BELT depending on whether I'm doing rough carpentry, drywall, or electrical work, and I finally found the perfect belt to hold them—a skindiver's weight belt. These belts are made of nylon webbing, so they are plenty tough. Even so, my belt is comfortable, even when I'm bending or stretching, because I can adjust it up or down on my waist and hips with the quick-release buckle.

—Michael Sweem, Downey, Calif.

Simple Sawhorse

WITH ALL THE FANCY SUBSTITUTES FOR WOODEN SAWHORSES, the real thing is sometimes overlooked. The sawhorse shown in the drawing at right is easy to build and sturdy enough to carry heavy loads. You can pound one together in about 20 minutes, so you don't need to worry about leaving them unattended on the site at night.

The sawhorse is built entirely of 2x4s, with whatever dimensions that suit you best. The two pieces assembled as an inverted T give it rigidity, allow the legs to flare equally, and provide a sturdy nailing surface.

—Swami Govind Marco, Montreal, Quebec

Nail-Pouch Chisel Roll

MANY LUMBERYARDS GIVE AWAY CANVAS NAIL APRONS. While the aprons may be flimsy and of little value as nail holders, they can be easily modified into a rollup tool pouch for auger bits or chisels. As shown at right, sew some seams into the pouches, and you've got slots to store and protect your edge tools.

—Samuel D. Jannarone, Upper Nyack, N.Y.

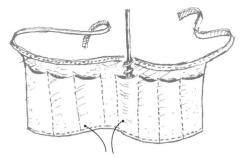

Seams in pouches make slots for bits or chisels.

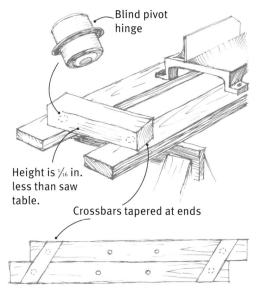

Blind pivot hinge

Height is ¹⁄₁₆ in. less than saw table.

Crossbars tapered at ends

Folded for transport

Folding Chopsaw Bench

HERE'S A DESIGN FOR A FOLDING STAND that I made for my power miter box. I started with a couple of 2x boards that I draped across a pair of sawhorses as shown in the drawing at left. I centered the saw on the boards and drilled holes for bolts that anchor the saw to the bench. Then I cut a pair of 4x4s to the right length for crossbars and ripped them to a thickness ¹⁄₁₆ in. shy of the height of the miter-saw table. I also tapered their ends so that in the folded position the crossbars remain flush with the boards.

I had some blind pivot hinges left over from a job, so I used them to attach the crossbars to the boards. But a countersunk machine screw or a lag bolt would work just as well.

—Roger Willmann, Columbia, Ill.

Ladder Sack

WHEN I CLIMB UP A LADDER TO WORK, I never have enough room for all my tools and accessories. To solve this problem, I screwed a leather pouch on the side of my ladder. I used one with a high inside pocket and cut out its bottom seam, which turns it into a drill holster. Now my ladder does double duty by carrying me and my tools.

—Will Milne, San Francisco, Calif.

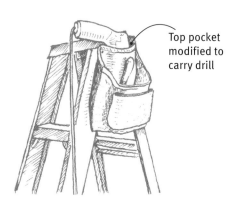

Top pocket modified to carry drill

Toolbox Runners

THE CORRUGATED PLASTIC LINER covering my pickup's bed helps to keep the finish in good shape, but its slick surface caused my toolboxes to slide from side to side whenever I turned corners. To make the boxes stay put, I made runners for them out of ½-in. dowels wrapped with ¾-in. rubber hose, as shown in the drawing at right. After drilling pilot holes, I affixed the runners to the bottoms of the boxes with three or four screws each, driven from the inside of the box. Now my boxes can hang on tight on the way to the job.

—David Gloor, Mountain Home, N.C.

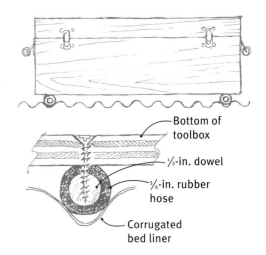

Bottom of toolbox

½-in. dowel

¾-in. rubber hose

Corrugated bed liner

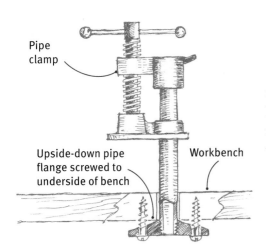

Pipe clamp

Upside-down pipe flange screwed to underside of bench

Workbench

Pipe-Clamp Hold-Down

WHENEVER I NEED A HOLD-DOWN CLAMP ON MY BENCH, I reach for one of my pipe clamps. As shown in the drawing at left, I insert a short length of pipe through a hole in the bench top. It is threaded into a pipe flange secured upside-down to the underside of the bench, giving me the versatility of a hold-down without having to buy one.

—Joseph Kaye, Uniondale, N.Y.

Saw Hangup

THE MUCH-ABUSED CIRCULAR SAW often ends up lying in the mud next to the sawhorses between cuts. Not only is this hard on the saw, but the endless bending and stooping to put the saw down and pick it up again is also hard on the back. One day I watched my brother staple a short length of 1x2 to the leg of his sawhorse to act as a saw hanger, and I've been doing the same ever since.

—Mark White, Kodiak, Alaska

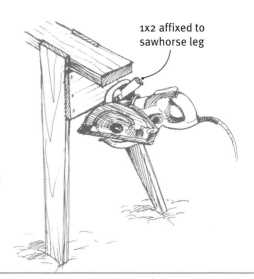

1x2 affixed to sawhorse leg

Knock-Down Saw Stand

My work as a remodeler requires that I carry a wide variety of tools and materials to the job, so space in the truck is at a premium. That's why I came up with the knock-down saw stand as shown in the drawing at right. The stand is constructed of 2x4 legs that have been connected in pairs by way of 2x4 crossbars. Screws and glue hold them together. The crossbars are notched in the middle where they engage one another.

I mounted my portable saw on a ¾-in. plywood base that has a big hole in its middle to evacuate sawdust. The saw is held fast to the stand during use by dowels. A pair of ⅜-in. holes along the front edge of the base corresponds to the dowels in the front legs of the saw stand.

—Robert Conrad, Pellston, Mich.

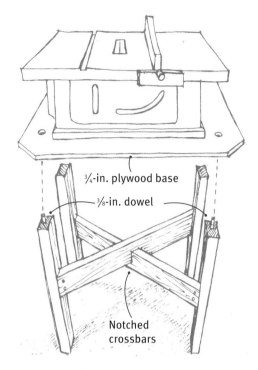

¾-in. plywood base

⅜-in. dowel

Notched crossbars

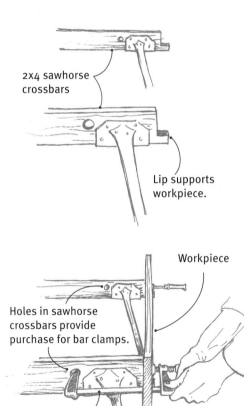

2x4 sawhorse crossbars

Lip supports workpiece.

Workpiece

Holes in sawhorse crossbars provide purchase for bar clamps.

Bar clamp

The Improved Sawhorse: It Has Lips

My work as a carpenter who specializes in repairing and replacing exterior trim means that I spend a lot of time fussing with long workpieces that have to be planed to fit. As shown in the drawing at left, I made some simple modifications to my sawhorses to make the planing go a little easier.

First, I cut the ends of the sawhorse crossbars to create little liplike ledges on their ends that are wide enough to support a piece of 1x stock on edge. And second, I bored 1-in.-dia. holes in the sawhorse crossbars to accommodate the stationary jaw of a bar clamp.

To use, I simply rest the workpiece on the horse's lips, clamp the stock to the crossbars, and plane away.

—John Michael Davis, New Orleans, La.

Sliding Tool Chest

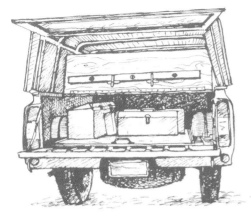

I WAS ABLE TO SOLVE THE PROBLEM of keeping my tools locked up and yet accessible in my pickup camper shell with the sliding-shelf tool locker.

I mounted a piece of angle iron along each side of the bed, level with the top of the tailgate. Then I cut a ¾-in. plywood shelf about 4 ft. long and as wide as the bed, and bolted it to the angle. I hinged another piece of plywood at the back of this where it would fold down just behind the wheel wells. I added a latching hasp and now had a lockable compartment for my tools as well as a storage space above them. For inside this compartment, I cut ¾-in. plywood narrow enough to slide between the wheel wells. I edged the plywood on three sides to keep toolboxes from sliding off, put a handle on the front, and attached casters to the bottom. This gave me a drawer that could be locked in place when the lid was closed. With the tailgate open, this sliding shelf will reach far enough to give access to everything on it.

Long material can be carried out the back of the camper shell supported by the top of this locker and the tailgate, which are at the same height. The entire system can be removed in minutes if the full use of the bed is needed. Also, I have discovered that the inside of the lid is a good place to store such awkward tools as my 4-ft. level.

—Kevin Ireton, Dayton, Ohio

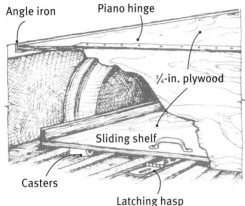

Angle iron
Piano hinge
¾-in. plywood
Sliding shelf
Casters
Latching hasp

I-Joist Sawhorse

THE DRAWING AT RIGHT SHOWS THE DETAILS of a new breed of sawhorse that we're building with our leftover I-joists. The sawhorses are light and strong, and they take about 20 minutes to assemble. They're so strong that we made an 8-ft. set for cutting rafters.

As shown in the drawing, I make the legs out of 1x4s, 33 in. long. The legs have compound miters on their ends that splay the legs out at a 3-in-12 pitch. From the side, the legs angle outward at 14°. The legs abut the bottom of the joist's top flange. They are cross-nailed through the plywood web, and the protruding nail points are clenched over to lock them in place. Along the bottom flange, 2x4 blocks provide the other nailing surface for the legs. Each of these nailed connections is reinforced with construction adhesive.

By the way, if you let the bottom flange run a little long, you've got a handy hook for hanging your circular saw.

—Steve Hill, Benicia, Calif.

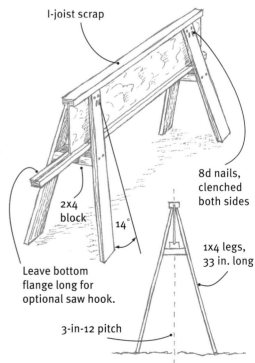

I-joist scrap
8d nails, clenched both sides
2x4 block
14°
1x4 legs, 33 in. long
Leave bottom flange long for optional saw hook.
3-in-12 pitch

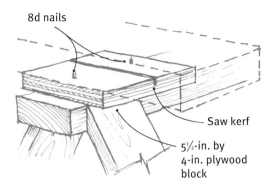

8d nails

Saw kerf

5½-in. by
4-in. plywood
block

Sawhorse Anchors

WHEN I HAVE TO RIP LONG PIECES OF 2x FRAMING LUMBER with a circular saw, I use a pair of ¾-in. plywood blocks to help me secure the work. The blocks are the same width as the lumber being cut. For instance, the 5½-in. block shown in the drawing at left is for a 2x6. I tack each block to a sawhorse with two 8d nails, leaving the head of the nail about ¼ in. above the block. Then I snip each nail head off with a pair of side cutters. This leaves about ⅛ in. of nail shank protruding from the block. These protrusions are sharp enough to penetrate a piece of softwood and long enough to hold it in place while I make my rip cuts. I set the blade depth so the cut enters the block, but not the sawhorse.

—P. J. Woychick, Boise, Idaho

Knock-Down Horses

I LIKE THE CONVENIENCE OF KNOCK-DOWN SAWHORSES. The commercial ones are generally too flimsy, and their small legs sink into the mud after you've got them loaded. After a lot of experimentation, here's how I build a strong, compact, stackable, knock-down sawhorse that doubles as a toolbox, as shown in the drawing at right.

I use a 2x8 or a 2x10 for the top. This gives me a bench surface that I can work on or set my miter box on. I cut a hand hole in the top for moving the horse around when it's set up.

The end caps, central dividers, and interior leg supports are 2x6s. The dividers hold a dowel that serves as a handle when the horse is disassembled and inverted. The compartment that is formed by these dividers should be the length of the legs so that they can be stored there, along with a few tools that you want to bring along.

The slots for the legs are ¾ in. by 5½ in., a snug fit for the 1x6 legs. I drill a pilot hole through the legs and the ⅝-in. plywood sides so that I can use a 16d nail to hold the legs to the body of the sawhorse when it's in use.

I cut different-length legs for different tasks, and I build different-width horses as well so that they stack easily. Aside from being slightly heavy, there's only one drawback to these sawhorses—you can't leave them on the job.

—George M. Payne, Olney, Md.

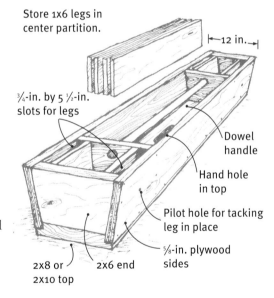

Store 1x6 legs in
center partition.

12 in.

¾-in. by 5 ½-in.
slots for legs

Dowel handle

Hand hole
in top

Pilot hole for tacking
leg in place

⅝-in. plywood
sides

2x8 or
2x10 top

2x6 end

Folding Workbench

WHEN I LEFT MY AMATEUR STANDING for an apprenticeship in carpentry, I also left my overbuilt workbench in the basement. One evening, when I was glancing over plans for site-built roof trusses, I realized that the same principles could be used to design a solid, easy-to-carry bench. Glued-on gussets are the secret. They reinforce a lightweight frame where it's needed most—at the joints. For my bench's frame I used 1x4 clear pine. At first I had my doubts about the strength of ¾-in. stock, but I'm glad now that I didn't use 2x4s.

I started by cutting four 29-in. legs, knowing that I'd probably shorten them. Then I cut four 13-in. rails, as shown in the drawing at right. This gives a finished width of 20 in. for the end frames. This might seem too narrow, but the bench is very stable in use. The top rails join flush to the top of the legs, and the bottom rails are 6 in. above floor level. This allows plenty of length for trimming the bench to the correct height.

I fastened the end frames together temporarily with corrugated fasteners, coated the gussets with glue, and stapled them across the joints. Staples are fine for this; the strength comes from the glue.

I made the mid-frame 5 ft. long, but if I had to do it over, I'd up it to 5½ ft. The bench would be a little harder to maneuver through tight places, but the extra stability would be worth it. The mid-frame stiles are 16 in., to match the dimension between the rails of the end frames. To resist racking, I added a 1x2 brace at each corner of the mid-frame.

To join the three frames, I used pairs of old 2½-in., tight-pin butt hinges—a pair at each end—so that the whole thing folds flat for transport or storage. The hinge leaves on the end frames need to be furred out with plywood the same thickness as the gusset.

My bench top is made from a 4x8 sheet of ½-in. CDX plywood, cut in half lengthwise and laminated together with yellow glue. I glued the two crowned sides together to ensure that the finished piece stays flat.

Once the top was dry, I glued 1½-in. by 2-in. lipping on each long edge. This strengthens the plywood, holds the top in place, and provides a handy purchase for clamps. Register blocks at the end of the top keep it centered.

I've finally gotten its height to the right point for me—I'm 5 ft. 10 in. tall, and the bench is now 27½ in. I can plane comfortably on it, get a knee up to crosscut, and still avoid the backache of working on low horses.

—T. D. Culver, Cleveland Heights, Ohio

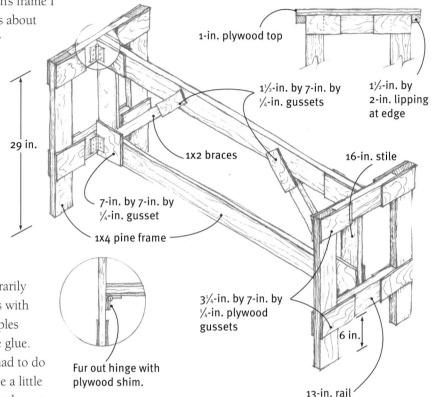

1-in. plywood top

1½-in. by 7-in. by ¼-in. gussets

1½-in. by 2-in. lipping at edge

29 in.

1x2 braces

16-in. stile

7-in. by 7-in. by ¼-in. gusset

1x4 pine frame

3¼-in. by 7-in. by ¼-in. plywood gussets

6 in.

Fur out hinge with plywood shim.

13-in. rail

Hurricane-Tie Sawhorse

I STOLE THE IDEA FOR THIS SAWHORSE from the local road crew, which uses a similar type of horse for its blockades. As shown in the drawing, the horses can be taken apart for transport and then quickly reassembled with the help of a screw gun. The knockdown connections are all made by way of metal framing connectors.

At the top of the 2x legs, a pair of hurricane ties accepts the crossbar. Below the crossbar, a rail screwed to joist hangers on the leg brace stiffens the horse.

These horses are strong, they can be made quickly, and they can be used for all kinds of applications, such as staging or miter-saw stands. I made a pattern out of hardboard that gives me the profile of the standard sawhorse. With the pattern, I can whip up a new set from wood scraps whenever or wherever I need a worktable.

—Michael DeYoung,
Chilliwack, British Columbia

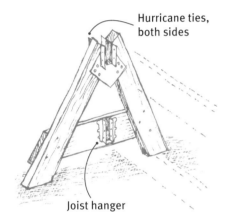

Hurricane ties, both sides

Joist hanger

Nailbag Liners

I SAVE HALF-GALLON MILK CARTONS, cut them in half, and use them for nail containers. Their 4-in. by 4-in. size fits nicely into the large bag on my nail pouch. When I'm done with one kind of nail, I remove the carton from the pouch and return it to its storage cabinet. This practice keeps the number of miscellaneous nails in my pouch from getting out of hand.

—Sam Francis, Bozeman, Mont.

3

Shortcuts, Tips & Tricks with Tools

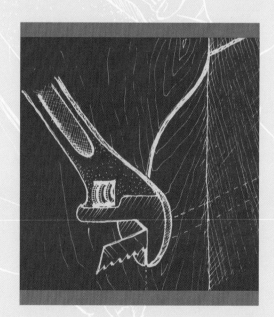

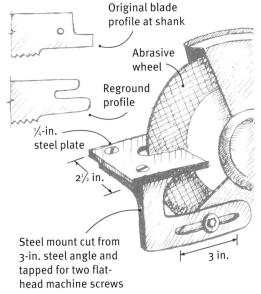

Original blade
profile at shank

Abrasive
wheel

Reground
profile

¼-in.
steel plate

2½ in.

3 in.

Steel mount cut from
3-in. steel angle and
tapped for two flat-
head machine screws

Born-Again Blades

ONE OF THE MOST ESSENTIAL REMODELING TOOLS is the reciprocating saw, but remolding work is very hard on their blades. Here are two tricks I use to prolong blade life.

First, I use 12-in. flexible blades whenever possible and do the cutting with the teeth closest to the tip. When the teeth wear down, I simply clip off the worn portion of the blade with tin snips and go back to work.

Second, and more important, I reshape broken shanks using a metal-cutting abrasive disc mounted on my bench grinder as shown in the drawing below. Outline the shape of an original blade on the broken shank and grind away the excess metal with the abrasive disc until the new shank fits snugly inside the saw's shoe. Then cut a slot in the blade just wide enough to accommodate the pin and retaining screw.

I've found innumerable uses for the bench grinder with this wheel installed. It will accurately cut a variety of materials from spring-steel roll pins to rubber hose. A work of caution: check the r.p.m. rating for the blade and the grinder to make sure they are compatible.

—Philip Zimmerman, Berkeley, Calif.

Tunneling Under Slabs

HAVE YOU EVER NEEDED TO BURY A WATER, GAS, OR ELECTRIC LINE and found your path blocked by a concrete slab? Here's a hydraulic method for making a small, accurate tunnel under such an obstacle, using a garden hose, iron pipe, and about $5 worth of common brass fittings from your hardware store.

Excavate a trench to the necessary depth, on both sides of the slab, and assemble the pictured fittings. It is important to maintain a level course under the slab, so be sure your trench is long enough to allow the pipe to remain level while the tunnel is being cut. If access is limited, short sections of pipe may be added with couplings as the tunnel gets longer. Sometimes it is best to work from both sides and meet in the middle.

The tapered nozzle delivers water at a very high velocity and quickly erodes the soil in its path. Adjusting the flow of water will control the diameter of the tunnel.

—Bruce Goodell, Oakland, Calif.

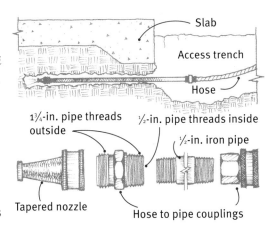

Slab

Access trench

Hose

1¾-in. pipe threads outside

½-in. pipe threads inside

½-in. iron pipe

Tapered nozzle

Hose to pipe couplings

Extruded Flashing

BENDING YOUR OWN FLASHING ON SITE usually produces wavy, crinkled pieces of sheet metal that make you wish you'd had them made up at a shop. Here's a fixture you can make on the site that produces near-perfect results.

Using a jigsaw or keyhole saw, cut the full-size cross section of the flashing you want to make into a plywood scrap that's at least 18 in. across. Nail the plywood across the studs of an unsheathed partition at chest level. Then cut a piece of roll flashing to length and insert it into one side of the cut in the plywood. With one person pulling and another supporting and feeding the flashing, this fixture makes the job easy.

—Mick Cappelletti, Newcastle, Maine

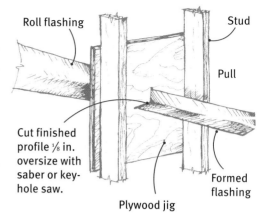

Roll flashing · Stud · Pull · Cut finished profile ⅛ in. oversize with saber or keyhole saw. · Plywood jig · Formed flashing

Cabinet Jack

INSTALLING HEAVY KITCHEN WALL CABINETS by yourself can be a dangerous juggling act. With the aid of a scissor jack, it's easy to keep them plumb and level long enough to install them. First, set the base cabinets. This leaves you with a working surface. Next, lay out level and plumb lines on the wall for the upper cabinets. Place a piece of scrap plywood on the top of the base cabinet and set the jack on the plywood. Then predrill the uppers for the stud layout, set the cabinet on the jack, and crank it into position.

To protect the casework from scratches, attach a 12-in. square piece of ¾-in. plywood to the bottom and top of the jack with countersunk flathead screws, and cover the plywood with carpet scraps. I fitted my jack sleeve with an old hole-saw arbor so that I can raise and lower the jack with my electric drill.

—Ron DeLaurentis, North Aurora, Ill.

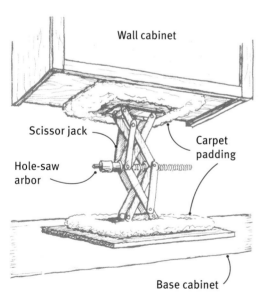

Wall cabinet · Scissor jack · Carpet padding · Hole-saw arbor · Base cabinet

A Sliding Dump-Bed

THE MOTHER OF THIS INVENTION is my hatred of shoveling aggregate out of my pickup truck. I built a shallow wooden box that keeps the stone in one place when I drive and dumps it exactly where I want it when I get to the site.

The dump-bed box fits between the truck's wheel wells, where it rests on two or three lengths of ¾-in. pipe. When the dump-bed is empty, I block it up with a couple of 2x4s to keep it from rolling around while I'm driving. Before loading, I pull out the blocks and make sure the pipes are oriented as shown in the drawing at right. This dump-bed holds about a half-yard, and the loader operators I've worked with so far have been able to fill it without spilling a granule.

To unload, I drop the tailgate all the way down, back the truck up to the dump point, and hit the brakes. The dump-bed rolls back, coming to rest with one end on the ground and the other on the back of the truck. I just pull out the end piece, and the rest of the aggregate can be pushed out of the dumper.

—Al Dorsa, Christiansted, St. Croix, V.I.

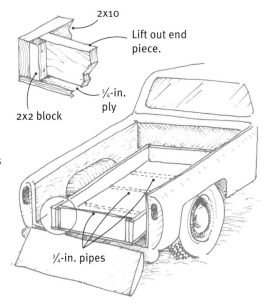

2X10

Lift out end piece.

¾-in. ply

2x2 block

¾-in. pipes

Utility-Knife Tune-Up

WHEN I WORK WITH DRYWALL, I find that the blade of my retractable-blade utility knife cakes up with gypsum dust, rendering the tool useless. To give the blade a longer working life, I take the handle apart and run the point of a soft graphite pencil over the blade and its guides. This removes any built-up gypsum particles, and at the same time deposits a layer of lubricating graphite that won't attract additional gypsum dust.

—Paul J. McCarthy, Hartford, Conn.

Squeaky Subfloor Fix

TO QUIET SQUEAKS IN FLOORS, I use a small joist block sistered to the original post, as shown in the drawing at left. Once I've located the squeak, I put a good bead of construction adhesive along the top edge of a block that is the same depth as the existing joist. With the block in the same place, I use a small jack in the crawl space to press it tightly against the subfloor. With the block nailed off and the jack removed, the job is done.

—Ross Fulmer, Atascadero, Calif.

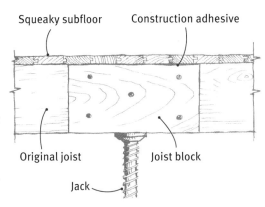

Squeaky subfloor   Construction adhesive

Original joist   Joist block

Jack

Router-Bit Storage

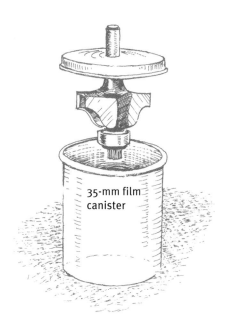

35-mm film canister

GOOD ROUTER BITS ARE EXPENSIVE, and it makes me cringe to think of their finely honed edges bumping together in a toolbox drawer. To protect my bits, I store them individually in plastic 35-mm film canisters. As shown in the drawing at left, I drill a hole in the lid the same size as the shaft of the router bit. Then I slip the lid over the shaft of the bit and snap it tight onto the canister. The cutting edges of the bit are protected, and I don't have to worry about storing them in my toolbox. I like to use clear canisters, such as those used for Fuji film, because they allow me to easily identify the bit without a label. These little containers work great for bits under 1⅛-in. diameter. Forstner and multispur bits can also be stored in them.

—Bruce Lowell Bigelow, San Francisco, Calif.

Removing Reluctant Fasteners

FOR THOSE AMONG US WHO LIKE TO RECYCLE WOOD, the perpetual problem is getting the embedded fasteners out of the wood. Some of the nails and screws have rusted right into the wood fibers, and pulling them is impossible because they've lost their heads long ago. To dig them out without making a mess of the surrounding material, I turn to my home-made hole saw. As shown in the drawing at right, I use a hacksaw and a triangular file to put teeth on the end of a length of ¼-in. steel pipe. Then I use a reamer to give the teeth a little set.

If you don't have a length of ¼-in. steel pipe, you can use copper pipe instead. Better yet, try a push rod. The best hole saw I've made so far started out as a push rod from a diesel engine. I cut the rod in half and put teeth on the hollow center section of the rod. The steel is thin and takes a sharp edge.

—Don Stevenson, Woodland, Wash.

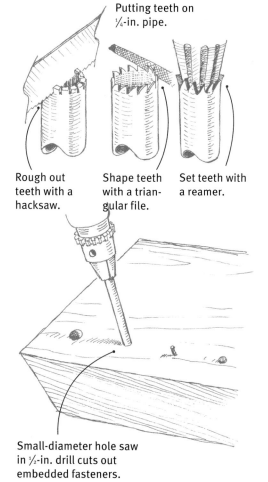

Putting teeth on ¼-in. pipe.

Rough out teeth with a hacksaw.

Shape teeth with a triangular file.

Set teeth with a reamer.

Small-diameter hole saw in ½-in. drill cuts out embedded fasteners.

Shingle Cheater

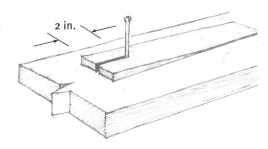

HERE'S A TRICK AN OLD CARPENTER SHOWED ME after watching me drive 16d galvanized casing nails, overhead, into 2x6 vertical-grain fir. I had just missed the nailhead, producing a deep hammer track in the board, and I was about to turn the air blue with a few choice phrases when he showed me how to make a cheater. He took a shim shingle and cut a lengthwise slot into the middle of the butt end. Once he had started the nail, he slipped the kerfed shingle around the shank of the nail, as shown, and invited me to hammer away. After that, when I missed the nail, the shingle took the hit, not the trim.

—Jeff Head, Port Angeles, Wash.

Cleaning Foam Off the Walls

I USE FOAM INSULATION FROM AN AEROSOL CAN when insulating around rough window and door openings. The next day, I trim all the excess foam away from the wall and the window frame with a mastic trowel, as shown in the drawing at left. Its serrated edges saw through the foam, leaving the foam flush with the wall.

—Keith Metler, Highland Park, Ill.

Improved Tool Grip

I'VE TAKEN TO WRAPPING THE HANDLES of my hand-held power tools and air nailers with tennis-racket grip tape. The tape provides a much better grip than bare metal, especially on hot, sweaty days. The tape allows you to hold the tool securely and safely without squeezing too hard, which helps avoid tendinitis (tennis elbow).

—Juris Pukinskis, Storrs, Conn.

Power-Tool Belt Clip

HAVE YOU EVER WANTED TO HOLD A NAIL GUN OR A POWER TOOL on your tool belt while working? Here's a rig that is easy to assemble, doesn't get in the way, and won't accidentally come loose from the belt. And with it, I can remove a tool from my belt faster than Wyatt Earp could have using just one hand.

As shown in the photo at right, I use a bent-gate carabiner as a hook to hang on a steel hammer loop. Carabiners are like a link of chain that can be opened by way of a spring-loaded leg. Rock-climbing stores stock them. I thread the carabiner onto a length of 1-in. webbing that is then tied at the ends to make a loop. For this I use a webbing knot that is known variously as a water knot, a ring bend, or an overhand bend. To secure the carabiner to the tool, I pass the loop of webbing around the tool's handle and then through itself.

—Cliff Tillotson, Santa Barbara, Calif.

Right-Angle Plugs for Tools

IT'S ALWAYS BEEN FRUSTRATING FOR ME when a power tool pulls loose from my extension cord. I've used twist-lock connectors, but they're bulky and hang up on things even more than a standard socket does. I've solved this problem by putting right-angle plugs on the cords to my tools, as shown in the drawing at left. Because they're not on the same axis as the socket, right-angle plugs are a lot harder to pull out. These plugs are available at hardware stores with or without a ground connector. In my area, the plugs cost between $1 and $7.

—Bob Francis, Napa, Calif.

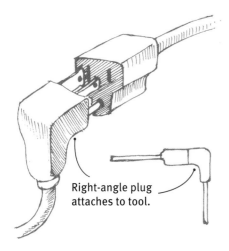

Right-angle plug attaches to tool.

Steady That Bob

IF YOU HAVE TO USE A PLUMB BOB on a windy day, dangle it in a pail of water to dampen its sway.

—Joe Graczyk, Cazadero, Calif.

Plumbing Posts

WHEN I SET POSTS, I used to find it awkward first to plumb one face, then the one next to it. One side was always getting a little out of adjustment. Now I use two levels strapped to adjacent faces of the same post, as shown. For a 4x4 post, a 20-in. tarp strap is the right length to secure my two levels. Now I have enough hands to set the post, and my level isn't on the ground when I need it.

—Patrick Lawson, Sooke, British Columbia

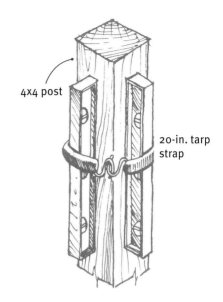

4x4 post

20-in. tarp strap

Slick Tips

AS A CARPENTER LIVING AND WORKING ON THE OREGON COAST, I have always found it a challenge to keep my saws and tape measures clean, dry, and free of sand and grit. Sand is hard enough on tools and equipment. Add rain, sawdust, salt, and wood sap, and you've got a real abrasive nuisance.

I found that liberal doses of silicone spray applied to my fully extended tape measures make them last two or three times longer than usual. Silicone spray coats smoothly, dries cleanly, and leaves surfaces slick. Oil-based sprays dry out and leave a greasy film. Spraying the shoe and blade of my circular saw makes for smooth, clean, and fast cuts. Ditto for table saws.

—Terry Mackey, Lincoln City, Ore.

Marking Tile

CHINA MARKERS, OR GREASE PENCILS, work great for marking tile for wetsaw cuts. They make a pretty wide line, but the lines won't wash off without some scrubbing. You can get grease pencils at office or art supply stores.

—Gene Swanson, Minneapolis, Minn.

More Praise for Masking Tape

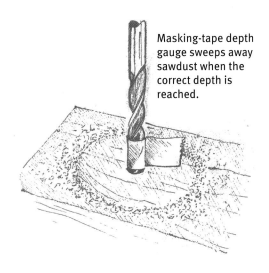

Masking-tape depth gauge sweeps away sawdust when the correct depth is reached.

I TOO HAVE USED MASKING TAPE in all the various ways that Herrick Kimball describes, plus a couple of others. For example, I use it to make labels on short lengths of electric cable. Before coiling them for storage, I mark their lengths on the strip of masking tape that keeps the coil from unwinding. Thus marked, it's easy to find a suitable hunk of wire without unnecessary unraveling. Masking tape is also good for clamping awkward pieces during glue-up. I mended a badly splintered chair spindle by gluing it and wrapping it with masking tape. Once the glue on the spindle cured, I sanded and painted it. That was 15 years ago, and the patch is still invisible. But my favorite use of masking tape is as a depth gauge. As shown in the drawing, I wrap it around the drill bit like a flag, with the ends sticking out. Then I bore my hole until the tape flag starts to sweep away the sawdust.

—K. Burt, Corvallis, Ore.

Foolproof Fluting

I HAD TO MAKE SOME FLUTED COLUMNS for a fancy entry. Flutes are typically milled using a core-box bit in a router with a guide mounted to one side. But a router will sometimes wander a bit when used with a single guide, and flutes have to be straight as pool cues, or they look awful. As shown in the drawing at right, I eliminated the problem by adding a second guide.

I put a 1-ft.-long 1x1 extension on each guide to ensure good bearing along the edge of my workpiece. Then I linked the two guides with a pair of 20-in. steel rods. I used a couple of sprinkler control rods with their ends cut off. They fit just fine. Trapped between the two guides, the router couldn't veer off course.

I held the workpiece in place with a 1x2 at each end. The 1x2s also acted as stops at the end of the router's pass. I set the spacing, ran the router down the board, turned the router around, and went back down the other side of the board. Then I reset the spacing and repeated the passes. This method is surprisingly quick and accurate.

—Gerret Wikoff, Los Angeles, Calif.

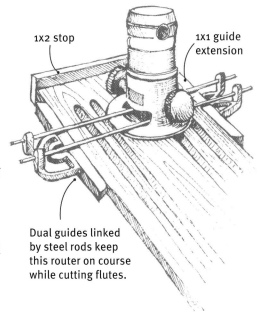

1x2 stop

1x1 guide extension

Dual guides linked by steel rods keep this router on course while cutting flutes.

Solo Window Installation

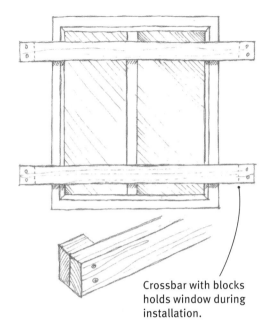

Crossbar with blocks holds window during installation.

I WAS RECENTLY FACED WITH INSTALLING WINDOWS in a new house, all by myself. Here's how I did it. First I cut a couple of 2x4s about 8 in. longer than my widest window. Then I measured the distance that the windows projected from the house and cut four blocks equal to this distance plus ¼ in. I screwed one block to the ends of each 2x4.

Working from the outside, I installed one of the vinyl windows and placed the 2x4s over it. I screwed the 2x4s to the wall on both sides of the window, as shown in the drawing at left. Now I was free to go inside and level the bottom of the window and center it in its opening with shims. The extra ¼ in. allowed me to move the window without interference from the 2x4 crossbars. When the window was centered and level, I went back outside and nailed it in place, beginning with the bottom flange. Then I pulled out the crossbars and moved on to the next window.

—Scott Bruce, Grand Blanc, Mich.

Corrugated Concrete Chute

WHEN THE READY-MIX TRUCK RUNS OUT OF CHUTE, it's easy to extend your reach with the site-built job shown at right. It's made of corrugated steel roofing that has been nailed to two flat 2x6 stringers and bent into a U shape. It maintains its profile with the help of 2x4 ties nailed across the top, and it is secured to the truck chute with a length of chain. Wet concrete is mighty heavy, and I consider 2x6 stringers to be the absolute minimum. My 16-ft. chute is strung on 2x10s, but it's somewhat overbuilt.

Without the 2x4 ties, the chute can be used as a slide for concrete blocks, as the corrugations eliminate much of the drag. Sure beats using a wheelbarrow.

—Al Dorsa, St. Croix, V.I.

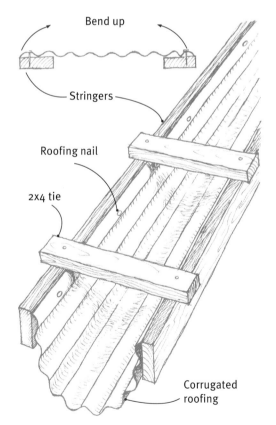

Bend up

Stringers

Roofing nail

2x4 tie

Corrugated roofing

Cutting Glass

HERE IS AN EASY WAY TO ENSURE A CLEAN BREAK when you have to trim just a bit off a piece of glass. First, find a straight piece of 2x4 that is at least as long as the piece of glass that needs to be trimmed. Next, cut a groove in the edge of the 2x4 that is just wide enough to accept the glass without being forced and deep enough to reach the scored line on the piece of glass.

After scoring the glass, slip it into the 2x4 and align its edge with the score mark. Lift up on the 2x4, as shown in the drawing at right, and the glass should break evenly right where you want it to. Be sure to wear gloves and eye protection whenever you work with glass.

—James E. Mitchell, Pentwater, Mich.

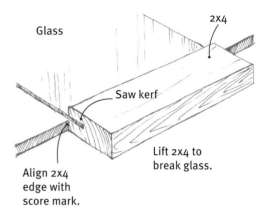

Glass

2x4

Saw kerf

Lift 2x4 to break glass.

Align 2x4 edge with score mark.

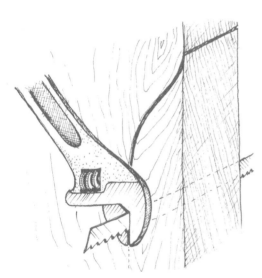

Blade Guide

A ROLLING BANDSAW is a good way to cut curves in heavy timbers, but if the timber is already part of the house, you've got to take the saw to the wood. We had to remove 3 in. from a 6x10 post to gain room for a stairway, and we used a Sawzall to make the cut. We guided the blade on the open side with a wrench as shown in the drawing at left. This operation takes two people and a fair amount of time, but it works very well.

—Jeff Morse, Tomales, Calif.

Warming Caulk Tubes

WHEN THE WEATHER TURNS ICY up here in New Hampshire, construction adhesives and caulks get so cold they won't budge out of their tubes. To prevent this, I installed a metal can (about one gallon in size) under the hood of my truck. I placed it near, but not quite touching, the engine. The lidless can has enough room in it for five tubes of caulk or adhesive. On my drive to work in the morning, the tubes warm up enough to allow their contents to flow easily. Depending on how cold it is, the heat from the mass of the engine block keeps them warm for several hours.

—Brian Carter, Concord, N.H.

Recycled Glue Bottle

As a carpenter who does primarily finish work, I go through a lot of yellow glue. The only economical way to buy it is by the gallon. Of course, you have to pour it into a smaller glue bottle to use it. Like most carpenters, I have a problem with losing the little cap that comes on small glue bottles. So the empty mustard bottle that turned up in our kitchen is the ideal glue bottle for my money. Plastic mustard bottles come in different sizes, and the cap is integral with the nozzle. Just give it a twist to open or close the bottle.

To be safe, I wrapped the bottle with duct tape and prominently labeled it as a GLUE BOTTLE. That way I won't have some momo framing carpenter accidentally squirting what he thinks is a gob of mustard on his lunch meat.

—Brian Kenney, Newport, R.I.

Triangle-Square Holder

One of the most useful tools invented in the last couple of decades is the triangle square. On the other hand, it is also one of the most awkward tools to carry on a standard tool belt. Losing your triangle square when you need it is frustrating, and, at heights, it can be dangerous. After spending years of jury-rigging various triangle-square holders, I have finally devised a simple and lightweight triangle-square holder that works well.

As shown in the photo at left, the holder is composed of a 16-in. length of sturdy belt leather. I used a couple of small panhead bolts and T-nuts to affix the ends of the loop to my leather hammer holder.

Then, I put a third bolt farther back through the side pouch to keep the loop from rotating downward at the back. My triangle-square holder is both simple and effective.

—Will Ruttencutter, Chico, Calif.

Quiet the Singing Ladder

If you're running down the road with howling ladders atop the truck, you might want to try this trick. Squirt a dab of expanding polyurethane foam into the ends of the ladder rungs. Plugged-up rungs keep out the wind, eliminating the annoying hum of the high-speed extension ladder.

—Joey Kaylor, Floyd, Va.

Reinforced Power Cords

THE FIRST THING TO FAIL ON EVERY POWER TOOL I've ever owned is the tapered-rubber strain relief that feeds the power cord into the tool. The large flexible tail breaks off, and eventually the wires break or short, putting the tool out of service. Official factory replacements are not always stocked locally, and they are often expensive. Recently, after doing a major tune-up on my truck, I discovered a handy, inexpensive alternative to the factory replacements—the rubber spark-plug boots used on many modern engines. After the spark-plug wire has been pulled out of the boot, most any power cord can be pushed through the center hole with the help of a little silicone spray. The flanged end can be carved with a utility knife to fit just about any tool mount. The result is a flexible, durable strain relief that costs nothing. I've fitted them with success to my sidewinder, trim, chop, and portable table saws. If your car or truck doesn't use this style of spark-plug boot, check at your local auto-repair shop for their throwaways.

Power cord

Spark-plug boot

Shape this end to fit tool mount

—Fred Staal, Isleton, Calif.

Documenting Projects

I HAVE A SIMPLE, ACCURATE WAY to document the placement of the framing, wiring, and plumbing parts that go into a construction project: photographs. If I see the possibility of future remodeling, or special use for a particular wall (such as carrying a row of cabinets), I photograph the wall before the drywall installation. If possible, I stretch a tape measure in a corner of the photograph to give me a scale. When excavation is part of the job, I take pictures of the water lines, septic systems, and other underground utilities.

Over the years I have saved many hours and avoided a lot of mistakes by referring to my photo file. When I am done with the job, I leave the photos with the owners in a package that includes the plans of their project.

—Howard Furst, Bellingham, Wash.

The Secret Life of Masking Tape

PEOPLE WHO USE MASKING TAPE just to keep paint from straying onto the wrong surface are missing out on some of its most useful characteristics. Masking tape is light in color, is cheap, and can be written on easily. These attributes make it ideal for various marking and layout applications. Here are some examples of how I use the stuff. By the way, I use the 2-in.-wide variety, and I don't worry about what brand it is.

Pencil marks on dark wood are tough to see, so I stick a piece of masking tape to the wood and make my mark on the tape. I do the same on glass or ceramic surfaces that don't take a pencil mark well. And if I need to make a reference mark on a stringline, I make a masking-tape flag on the string and make my mark on it.

You can make a removable chalkline on virtually anything—even carpet— by snapping the line on a strip of masking tape. If you've snapped a couple of misplaced lines on a surface, clear the picture by taping over them and beginning anew on a fresh run of masking tape.

When remodeling, I often tear out everything down to the bare studs. Then, to show clearly the placement of new electrical and plumbing components, I stretch a horizontal length of tape over the studs and map my locations on it.

I also make templates using masking tape and heavy paper. (I use manila folders because they're cheap, and they work well.) For example, if I need to cut out a complex sheet of ¼-in. underlayment for a bathroom floor, I'll make a pattern of the projections and indentations by taping pieces of paper together, as shown in the drawing at right.

Masking tape helps me organize. I'm always using it to label loose electrical wires. To keep small, yet important parts from getting lost, I wrap them in tape, label them on the outside, and stick them in a safe place.

Masking tape can be used as a clamp where nothing else will work. For example, to fix splits in delicate wood trim, I apply the glue and then wrap the trim with a piece of masking tape until the glue sets up. And when I'm tiling walls, I can keep a row of tile from slipping before the mastic sets with a strip of tape affixed to an anchorage above the tile.

—Herrick Kimball, Moravia, N.Y.

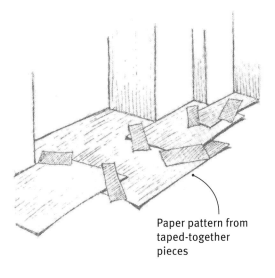

Paper pattern from taped-together pieces

Buzz, the Stud Locator

TRY USING AN ELECTRIC SHAVER to find studs in any wall. Simply buzz the shaver along the wall and listen for a distinct change in tone. It never misses.

—Jeffrey Fosbre, Dunellen, N.J.

Sawblade Jacket

I GET A LOT OF LITERATURE about building products. Much of it comes in heavy paper folders with pockets on the inside. After I've filed the literature in the proper drawer, I use the folders to protect my circular-saw blades. As shown in the drawing at left, blades tuck neatly into one of the interior pouches, protecting their teeth. The pouches are usually 9 in. wide—big enough for almost all the blades I typically use. With the blades tucked in the folders, I can store them like books on a shelf.

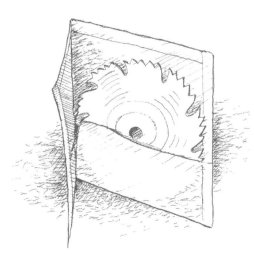

—Mark Feirer, Woodbury, Conn.

Talkin' Trash

I LINE MY SHOP VACUUM with a plastic trash bag to make it easier to empty without generating the clouds of dust ordinarily associated with dumping a vacuum's contents. To keep the bag from obstructing the vacuum's filter, I place a disposable cardboard basket inside the bag. The cardboard basket should be cut to a height of no less than three quarters of the canister height and should be of sufficient length to encircle at least one-half of the canister's circumference. This technique will also boost the suction in a vacuum with a leaky canister.

—Mark Genovese, Taunton, Mass.

Sherlock Ohms

WE RECENTLY HAD THE MISFORTUNE of finding a water pipe by running a nail through it. To make matters worse, the pipe was under a floor overlaid with tile backer board. Faced with blindly destroying the floor in search of the nail (the ceiling below was already finished), I hit on the idea of finding the leak electrically.

I got out my volt meter and set it to the resistance mode. I grounded one lead to a water pipe and then probed each nail head with the other lead. When I found the culprit nail, the circuit was complete (consult your electrician if you're at all in doubt about how this works). The happy result was that we were able to make a minimal hole in the floor for repairs.

—Jim Albertson, Longmont, Colo.

Table Saw Sanding Disk

Have you ever wished you had a disk sander? If you have a table saw, you've already got one. Simply grind the teeth off an old blade—if you have a 10-in. saw, a 12-in. blade with the teeth removed will likely fit. Stick a sanding disk onto the toothless blade with some contact cement, and you're ready to go. You can even use your miter gauge to assist in sanding different angles.

—Roger A. Bowyer, Daton, Ohio

Marking on Tile

As a professional tilesetter, I've occasionally used a grease pencil to mark my cuts. But I prefer another marker. My favorite is an aluminum knitting needle, which will leave a legible mark on all but the glossiest porcelains. And unlike the grease pencil, it leaves a very precise line. When the needle dulls, I sharpen it with a file, a sander, or a grinder. I've been using the same needle for over 20 years, and I haven't begun to wear it out.

—Ken Morrill, Corralitos, Calif.

Quick Clamp Support

One problem I have had in working on-site is not having a workbench to hold stock for edge planning and similar operations. I solved this by using a handscrew clamp and a C-clamp in combination, as shown in the drawing at right. The C-clamp secures one foot of the handscrew clamp to the leg of the sawhorse, leaving the other foot free for adjustment. This set-up works well on most conventional sawhorses.

—Ben Erickson, Eutaw, Ala.

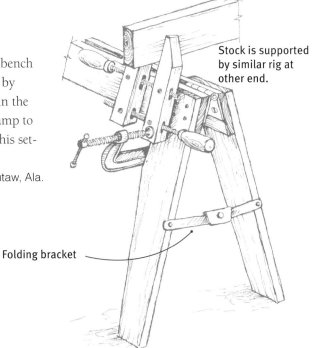

Stock is supported by similar rig at other end.

Folding bracket

4

Site-Built
Tools & Jigs

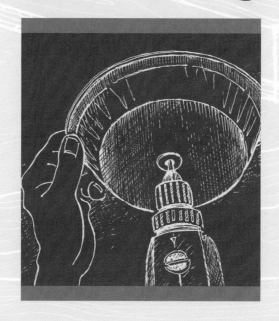

Panel Hook

A 4x8 SHEET OF DRYWALL, pegboard, or plywood can be a nuisance to carry. With my device, one person can easily maneuver these bulky panels. I fabricated the metal hook shown in the drawing at right from a scrap piece of 12-ga. cold-rolled steel. A short length of rope is threaded through the ½-in.-dia. hole and serves as an adjustable handle. By hitching up on the rope slightly and adjusting the panel's center of gravity I can negotiate stairs, up or down, with no problem.

—George Eckhart, Kenosha, Wis.

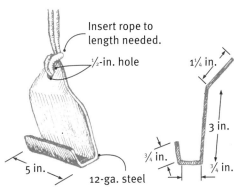

Insert rope to length needed.

½-in. hole

1¼ in.

3 in.

¾ in.

¾ in.

5 in.

12-ga. steel

Nail Pickup

HERE'S A REFINEMENT ON THE OLD IDEA of using a magnet on a string to pick up nails and other ferrous-metal debris on a job site. I placed a large horseshoe magnet inside a plastic container (mine originally held ricotta cheese). As shown in the drawing at left, I attached a string to the top of the magnet and fed it through a hole in the center of the lid. Then I put a couple strips of duct tape around the edge of the lid to keep it attached to the container. The result: a magnet that easily picks up metal, yet, at the jerk of the string, all bent nails, screws, and flashing snippets fall off and land in my recycling receptacle.

—Raja Abusharr, Eugene, Ore.

Clip-On Nail Set

I USED TO LOSE NAIL SETS CONSTANTLY. They always fell out of my nail bags while I was on the job. To solve the problem, I took a removable clip from a mechanical pencil and slipped it on my latest nail set. I haven't lost it yet.

—Greg Halverson, Eugene, Ore.

Steam-Bending on Site

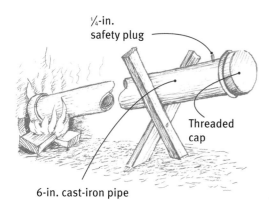

¼-in. safety plug

Threaded cap

6-in. cast-iron pipe

WHILE WE WERE RESTORING A LARGE VICTORIAN BUILDING in San Francisco, we had to bend a lot of redwood trim around 4-ft. and 12-ft. diameter framed partitions and enclosures. Steam-bending seemed like the easiest way to do this, but because the trim pieces were so long, we had to devise an equally long steamer to accommodate them.

I went to a scrap-metal yard and bought a 14-ft. length of 6-in. threaded cast-iron pipe for $25 (8-in. pipe was also available). I also bought two end caps. I put a thin layer of plumber's putty on the threads at one end of the pipe and tightly screwed on one of the caps. Near the opposite end, I drilled a ¼-in. safety-valve hole and tapped in a cedar plug. Then we put the capped end into the building's fireplace, built a fire around it with wood offcuts, and poured in about a gallon of water.

About 20 minutes later, the pipe was steaming, and I picked out four pieces of the redwood trim with the most vertical grain, shoved them inside, and screwed the second cap on hand-tight. After about another 20 minutes we uncapped the steamer, removed the wood (wearing gloves), and cut it quickly. The redwood easily bent to the required curves.

As we grew accustomed to the procedure, we precut the trim pieces because working time is short—about 3½ minutes. Experience also taught us that vertical-grain pieces were much easier to bend than flat-grain ones. With flat grain, the growth rings tend to separate during bending.

The advantage of this steamer is that 20-ft. lengths of trim can be steamed by joining two pieces of pipe with a union. Also, most job sites have scrap wood and a safe place to build a fire. The disadvantage is that cast iron stains redwood black. This isn't a problem if you're going to paint the trim.

—Michael Spexarth, El Cerrito, Calif.

Wind-Up Plumb Bob

IF YOU'RE TIRED OF WINDING THE STRING on your plumb bob, and you've get an empty spring-wound tape case lying around, try this. First, whittle a wooden plug to fill the tape slot and drill a hole in it a little larger than the diameter of the string you use. Now remove the old tape and tie your line to the end of the spring. Let the spring and some of the line retract into the tape case, thread the string through the hole in the plug, and press-fit the plug in place. Now tie a knot in the line or attach your plumb bob, and you're in business. You can get at least 25 ft. of line in a 25-ft. tape case, and with a larger-diameter line, the push lock will still work.

—Brent Lanier, Pleasant Gardens, N.C.

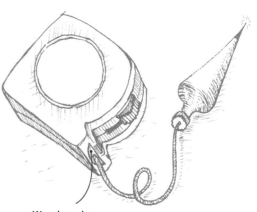

Wooden plug

Dustless Drilling

AFTER OUR COMPANY HAD PAINTED AND DECORATED the interior of an ornate 19th-century church, we had to install a new sound system. This meant drilling through a 20-in.-thick plaster and brick wall located directly over a gilded ornamental plaster arch. To prevent a disastrous mess of fine brick powder filtering down upon the arch, I devised the vacuum fitting shown in the drawing at right to contain and collect the dust.

The fitting consisted of a 3-in. diameter cardboard mailing tube about 8 in. long and a thin gasket of foam rubber to seal the space between the wall and the end of the tube. I cut a hole into the side of the tube to receive a vacuum hose, which I taped to the fitting for an airtight seal. As we drilled into the wall with a heavy-duty hammer drill and a 30-in. masonry bit, the dust was contained within the cardboard tube and immediately sucked up by the vacuum. The hole was drilled without a trace of dust reaching the arch.

—Jeff Kerbeykian, Rego Park, N.Y.

Foam-rubber gasket

Cardboard tube

Vacuum nozzle

Drill bit

¼ in.

Garage-door roller

3 in. o.c.

Saw-table height minus ⅛ in.

Plywood gusset

Outboard-Roller Stand

ONE OF THE MOST AWKWARD OPERATIONS to perform in my tiny one-man cabinet shop is crosscutting a full sheet of plywood. The outboard roller stand shown in the drawing at left has made this task a lot easier for me. The roller stand is essentially a sawhorse with a row of garage-door rollers mounted 3 in. on center across the length of the crossbar. I made my stand out of 2x4 stock, screwed and glued together for rigidity and braced at the top with plywood gussets. With one of these stands beside my table saw, I can push a sheet of plywood through a cut with little resistance.

—Lewis A Locke, Ellenburg, Wash.

Erasable Scratch Pad

IF YOU GLUE A SMALL PIECE OF VINYL SIDING to your tape measure, you'll always have a handy note pad for jotting down measurements. Once you're done with them, the numbers can be easily wiped off.

—Craig Horstmeier, Davis, Ill.

On-Site Vise

THE VISE SHOWN IN THE DRAWING at right is a handy and inexpensive tool for securing work up to 1¾ in. thick. It is made of 2x2s screwed and glued to a piece of ½-in. plywood. On the job site, I usually screw one to a subfloor, deck, bench, or sawhorse. The workpiece fits into the tapered slot between the 2x2s, and it's held fast by a 2x wedge driven into the gap. To level the workpiece, I shim its other end with a piece of ½-in. plywood. This rig works especially well for planing the edges of boards.

—Carl Meinzinger, Guemes Island, Wash.

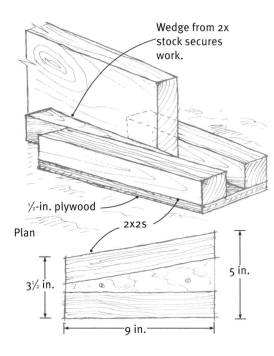

Wedge from 2x stock secures work.

½-in. plywood

Plan

2x2s

3½ in.

5 in.

9 in.

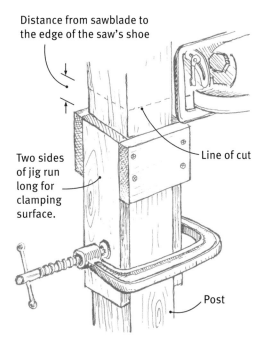

Distance from sawblade to the edge of the saw's shoe

Two sides of jig run long for clamping surface.

Line of cut

Post

Post Cutoff Jig

THIS YEAR WE HAVE BEEN DOING A LOT OF DECKS AND FENCES, and to simplify leveling the tops of all the posts I devised the jig that is shown in the drawing at left.

The post cutoff jig is a four-sided box with inside dimensions 1/16 in. larger each way than the cross section of the posts. The four sides of the box meet in the same plane at the top, where they are secured with screws. The two long, narrow sides hang down about 10 in. for a clamping surface.

First we plumb and stabilize all the posts, letting their tops run wild. Then we mark the desired height on one post and transfer that height to the rest using a water level. Below each mark we measure down and scribe a second mark. This measurement is equal to the distance from the sawblade to the edge of the saw's shoe.

Now we drop the jig over the post, clamp it so the top edge is on the lower mark, and use the top of the jig to guide the saw along all four sides of the post. If the piece that's being cut off is longer than 1 ft. or so, then have a helper lift up on it as you're finishing the cut so that it won't bind on the blade or fall on you.

—Timothy Pelton, Fairfield, Iowa

Epoxy Syringe

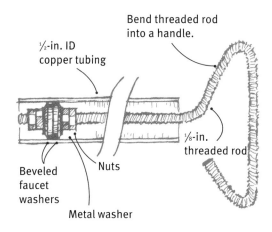

½-in. ID copper tubing

Bend threaded rod into a handle.

⅛-in. threaded rod

Beveled faucet washers

Nuts

Metal washer

MY CREW AND I HAVE BEEN ADDING A SECOND STORY to an older home, but before we could get to the framing we had to deal with the foundation. The original footing was too narrow to carry the weight of the addition, so we had to widen it by adding new footings alongside the old ones. To connect the old and new concrete, the engineer called for ¾-in. rebar dowels. And the dowels had to be epoxied into the old footings. I checked out the epoxy in glass capsules made for this situation, but at around $4 apiece they were more than we wanted to spend—we had hundreds of empty holes to fill. There are several batch mix epoxies also available for much less. The epoxy is thick enough to stay in a horizontal hole without drooling out before it sets up. A batch of it cures slowly—about a two-hour pot life at 65°F. But once in the pot, how to get it into the holes?

Our solution is shown in the drawing at right. It is a syringe made of a length of ½-in. ID copper tubing, with a plunger of ⅛-in.-dia. threaded rod. At one end of the rod, I made a piston out of a pair of beveled faucet washers. They are held fast by washers and nuts. Tightening the nuts increases the diameter of the piston a bit, ensuring a good fit. To fill the syringe with a dose of epoxy, put the tube in the pot and pull up on the plunger. Now you're ready to expel the adhesive into the target hole. Using this method, we bonded all the required dowels at a cost of about 75 cents apiece.

—Joe Wilkinson, Berkeley, Calif.

Sawblade Compass

AS I WAS ABOUT TO INSTALL A TOILET on a recent plumbing job, I made a discovery. I needed to draw a circular cutline on the subfloor for the toilet flange, but I didn't have a compass handy. I did have my Sawzall, though. I removed its blade and drove a nail through the hole in the blade into my center mark on the floor. With my pencil resting between two of the blade's teeth, as shown at left, I was able to draw a perfect circle—just the size I needed.

—Anthony Revelli, New York, N.Y.

Adjustable Cutoff Fixture

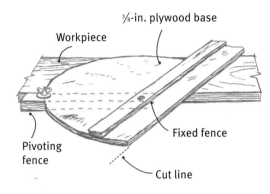

Workpiece

⅜-in. plywood base

Fixed fence

Pivoting fence

Cut line

I HAD TO CUT SOME ACUTE ANGLES on 11-in.-wide, 16-ft.-long oak planks. Rather than haul them back to the shop to use the radial-arm saw, I devised the cutting fixture shown in the drawing at left. It's basically a big version of the metal saw protractors I'd seen in mail-order catalogs, but the materials were practically free, and I didn't have to wait for the mail carrier to bring it.

The ⅜-in. plywood base is 32 in. long. I made the distance from its right edge to the fence a little wider than the distance from the edge of my saw's base to the blade. I used a fine-tooth blade to trim off the extra plywood with my circular saw, using the fence to guide the cut. That made the right edge of the base parallel with the fence. Cuts are aligned on this edge.

The circular portion of the plywood base has a 13½-in. radius. A 1x2 fence that pivots on a machine screw is mounted under the fixture. I covered the edge of the pivoting fence that bears against the workpiece with a strip of sandpaper to keep the jig from slipping off its layout line. Once I've got the angle between the pivoting fence and saw guide where I want it, I secure the fence to the base with a wing nut over a big washer.

—Brad Schwartz, Santa Ana, Calif.

Low-Budget Water Level

AN INEXPENSIVE WATER LEVEL can be made out of a clear plastic 1-gal. jug, a tubeless-tire valve stem (with guts and cap removed), and an appropriate length of clear vinyl tubing, as shown in the drawing at right. First, drill a hole that is sized to accept the valve stem approximately 2 in. up from the bottom of the jug. Insert the valve stem in the hole, fit one end of the tubing over the stem, and tape a ruler to the free end of the tubing to be used as a reference stick. Finally, fill the jug with water and add a few drops of food coloring to make the level easier to read.

Before using the level, be sure to bleed any air bubbles out of the tubing. And during use, keep the free end of the tubing above the level of the water in the jug to keep water from draining out the free end of the tube. Water levels are very accurate, and this one can be just the ticket for someone who doesn't need one often enough to justify buying a commercially manufactured one.

—Jeff Jorgensen, Tonopah, Nev.

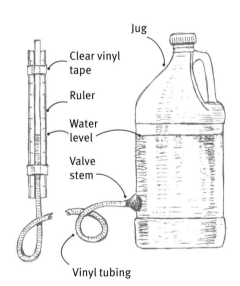

Jug

Clear vinyl tape

Ruler

Water level

Valve stem

Vinyl tubing

Miter Clamps in a Pinch

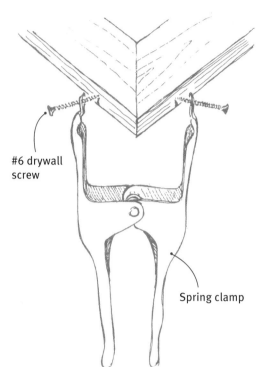

#6 drywall screw

Spring clamp

MITER CLAMPS (known as pinchdogs in our part of the Southwest) are mighty useful for putting pressure on a mitered frame during a glue-up or nailing session.

But miter clamps are not always easy to locate. As shown in the drawing, I make my own pinchdogs out of two components that can be obtained easily: spring clamps and drywall screws.

To make a pinchdog, I first center punch and drill $7/64$-in. holes in the jaws of a spring clamp. Rather than center the holes in the jaws, I put them a bit off-center.

This placement permits the clamp to reach a bit further and to grab the work at odd angles. The offset placement also allows me to use a couple of clamps at the same time if I need to apply extra pressure.

I run a #6 drywall screw into the holes in the spring-clamp jaws. The sharp points of the drywall screws will bite into almost any material.

—Sven Hanson, Albuquerque, N.M.

Door-Pull Jig

WHENEVER I NEED TO INSTALL PULLS on cabinet doors, I begin the job my making a jig to locate the screw holes. The jig, shown in the drawing at right, is a piece of plywood (¼ in. to ½ in. works fine) bordered on two sides by 1x2 fences that meet at 90°. Grooves in the 1x2s accept the plywood insert, creating a fence on both sides of the jig. Once I have decided where I want the pulls to be in relation to the corner of the cabinet doors, I drill corresponding holes in the plywood insert, as shown.

To use the jig, simply snug the fences against the corner of the cabinet door where you want to install the pull, and drill your holes using those in the plywood as a guide. For the adjacent door, flop the jig and you're ready to drill.

—Andrew George, Richmond, Va.

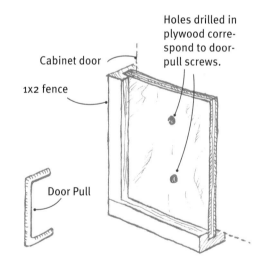

Holes drilled in plywood correspond to door-pull screws.

Cabinet door

1x2 fence

Door Pull

Leveling Rod

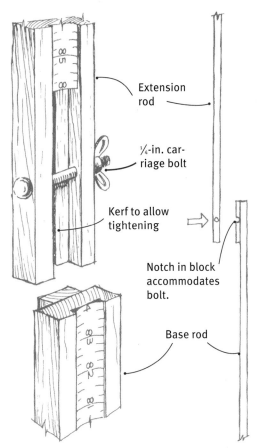

Extension rod

¼-in. carriage bolt

Kerf to allow tightening

Notch in block accommodates bolt.

Base rod

THE DRAWING AT LEFT ILLUSTRATES AN INEXPENSIVE DESIGN for an accurate, two-piece leveling rod made from a defunct 1-in.-wide tape measure. To make the base rod, begin with a piece of straight, knot-free 1x stock, ripped to a full 2-in. width. I think 7 ft. is a good length for this section of the rod. Use a router or a dado head to cut a ⅞-in.-wide by ¼-in.-deep groove in the base rod. Use tip snips to cut a 7-ft. section of tape, and press-fit the tape into the groove. It should stay put.

To make an extension rod, cut another groove in a similar piece of wood, an inch or so shy of 7 ft. long. At one end, deepen the groove to ½ in. for the first 5 in. of the rod and cut a saw kerf 5 in. in the center of the groove. Next, drill a hole for a ¼-in. carriage bolt, as shown in the drawing. Now you can press the continuing portion of the tape into the groove, starting at the end of the kerf.

At the top of the base rod, glue a ⅞-in.-wide block, about 5 in. long and ½-in. thick. This block has to be notched to accommodate the bolt in the extension rod. To use the extension, press the block at the top of the base rod into the groove in the extension rod. Adjust the extension up or down until its tape is even with the top of the base rod, and tighten the wing nut.

When the extension rod is not in use, I turn it upside down and reattach it to the base rod, out of the way. This rod is accurate, and I think it's easier to read than commercial ones, which cost $60 or more.

—Jim Reitz, Towson, Md.

Multipurpose Doorpull Jig

THE DRAWING AT RIGHT SHOWS A JIG I use for quickly locating the screw holes for cabinet pulls. In the application illustrated here, the jig is being used on a drawer front. The notch at the top of the jig is aligned with a pencil mark on a piece of tape that indicates the center of the drawer. Drawers of different depths require their pulls to be placed at different distances from their top edges—hence the series of holes.

To use the jig for locating pulls on cabinet doors, I rotate the jig 90° and align its edge with the door's top edge or some molded detail in the door. The jig is laid out with equal distances from its sides to the pullholes, allowing it to be flipped to do right-handed or left-handed doors.

—Mark Hallock, Capitola, Calif.

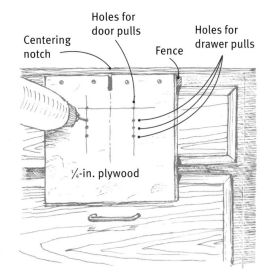

Centering notch

Holes for door pulls

Fence

Holes for drawer pulls

¼-in. plywood

Solo Overhead Drilling

IT'S TOUGH TO DRILL HOLES IN AN OVERHEAD STEEL BEAM. Here's a trick to simplify the process. The drill is sandwiched to the top of a 2x4 post by a pair of plywood cheeks affixed to a 2x4 block. A bracelet of three linked stainless-steel hose clamps holds the assembly together. The drill switch is held down to the on position (at medium speed) with a short length of soft wire. I turn the drill on and off via the plug on the extension cord, which I keep draped over my shoulder. The drilling speed is adjusted by the amount of pressure applied by the hydraulic floor jack. With one hand holding the post and the other applying pressure with the hydraulic jack, I can accurately position the bit.

—Joseph Fetchko, Ocean City, Md.

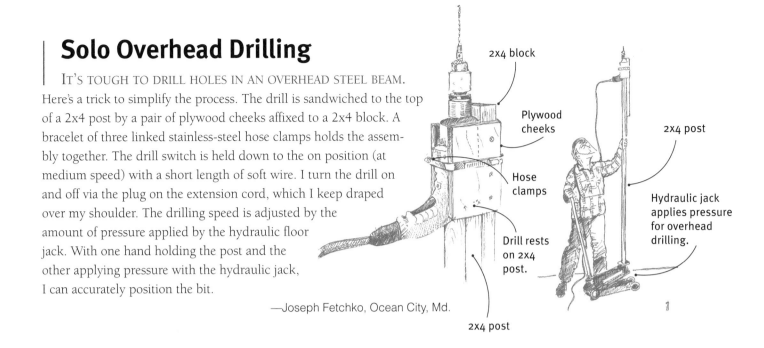

2x4 block

Plywood cheeks

2x4 post

Hose clamps

Drill rests on 2x4 post.

Hydraulic jack applies pressure for overhead drilling.

2x4 post

Magnet Helper

A MAGNET CAN BE A VERY HANDY TOOL around the shop or job site. When I'm working with brads or tacks, I use a magnet to keep them all concentrated in one place. The little nails will stick out like tiny thorns, making them easy to grab between two fingers.

Whenever I have to disassemble a tool and I'm liable to misplace a part in the surrounding sawdust, I get out a magnet to manage all of the parts. It saves a lot of time not having to look for lost screws.

—Ron Davis, Novato, Calif.

Stair-Button Rip Fence

WHEN I NEED AN ACCURATE RIP on a job site without a tablesaw, I use my stair-gauge fixtures. I clamp them on the front and back of my circular-saw baseplate, equidistant from the blade. This requires a saw with a flat baseplate. Measure the distance from the blade to the stair buttons just as you would with a rip fence, and then make the cut normally. With this quick setup, I get table-saw accuracy.

—Gred Gross, Wooster, Ohio

Storage Reel

THE FIRST THING I'VE ALWAYS DONE when I arrive on a site is roll out my cords from the meter loop to the day's work area. Next, I roll out my nail guns from the compressor to the area where they will be used. At the end of the day, the last thing I do is roll these same lines up and place them in my truck.

Up until about 10 years ago, this was always a time-consuming task. If I didn't make the effort to roll or braid these items neatly at pickup, the next day's rollout would be a tangle of 10-ga. cords and ⅜-in. hoses. Then one day I met a fellow with an outfit similar to the one shown in the drawing at right. It took him only about two minutes to roll and store about 300 ft. of cords and an equal length of air lines.

That evening, I made up my own reels using scrap ¾-in. CDX plywood, 3-in. schedule-40 PVC pipe, and a used lazy-Susan bearing. The pipe winding core is affixed to the plywood disks by way of a couple of plugs that I cut from 2x stock with a hole saw. I countersank the screws that secure the pipe to the plugs to keep the edges of the screw heads from abrading the cords.

On my cord reel, shown in the drawing at right, I have a 4-way outlet with 100 ft. of 10-ga. cord attached permanently. I find that this is usually sufficient to get me from the meter loop to my work area. My other extensions are attached end to end and rolled up on top of the permanent cord. The 4-way outlet allows me to run two saws at my main area and run two additional cords from that site to wherever they may be needed.

My hose reel simply has a hole in the top disk through which I pass the first hose end. This anchors the hose and keeps it from spinning on the core while I roll up 300 ft. of hoses connected end to end.

After nearly daily use, my original reels are still working well. The plywood disks have delam-inated a bit and the bearings have become a little sloppy, but that's okay. I wouldn't want this work to get too easy.

—Ric Winters,
Georgetown, Tex.

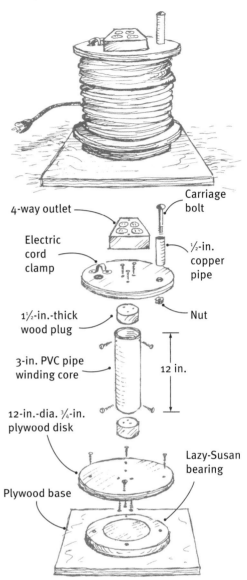

Carriage bolt

4-way outlet

Electric cord clamp

½-in. copper pipe

Nut

1½-in.-thick wood plug

3-in. PVC pipe winding core

12 in.

12-in.-dia. ¾-in. plywood disk

Lazy-Susan bearing

Plywood base

Shim-Cutting Jig

HERE'S A TABLE SAW JIG that you can use to make shims from scraps of wood. The base of the jig is a rectangular piece of plywood, with an angled notch cut out on the side that passes by the sawblade. The jig's handle is also wood, patterned after that of a handsaw. To make sure the shims stay in the jig's notch while cutting them, I screwed a hold-down cleat to the top of the jig, as shown in the top portion of the drawing at right. In use, I make a couple of passes with a piece of 1x stock and then flip the stock around to compensate for the tapered edge that's left over. With this jig I can quickly make shims that are more accurate than ready-made cedar shims or shingles.

—John Kraft, Oakland, Calif.

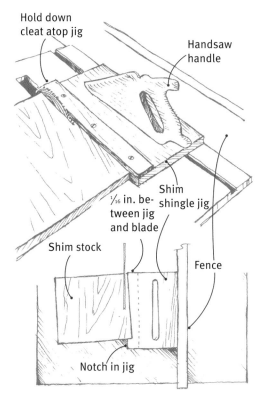

Hold down cleat atop jig

Handsaw handle

Shim shingle jig

1/16 in. between jig and blade

Shim stock

Fence

Notch in jig

Plan view, without hold-down

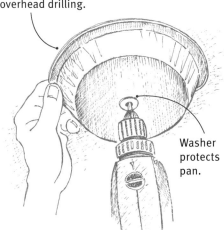

Aluminum pie pan catches debris from overhead drilling.

Washer protects pan.

Catch Dust from Overhead Drilling

WHEN DRILLING INTO A CEILING, you've got dust falling into your eyes, into the drill motor, and all over the client's floor. I prevent the problem with the trick shown in the drawing at left. I drill a ¼-in.-dia. hole in the center of a cheap aluminum pie pan and run my bit through the hole. To keep the bit from chewing up the hole in the pie pan, I glue a washer to its bottom to reinforce the opening. In use, I hold the edge of the pan to keep it from turning.

—Thomas K. Wilson, San Diego, Calif.

Shop-Vacuum Nozzle

I DO A LOT OF INTERIOR FINISH WORK. Sometimes the owners have already taken up residence, and the dust and chips created by my work can be a real nuisance. To gather up the mess that I make, I've been using a plastic bottle as a nozzle. As shown in the drawing at right, I cut the bottom off the bottle and angle the sides upward to resemble a scoop. Affixed to the hose with some duct tape, the scoop lets me easily pick up big and small debris at the same time.

—Michael Sweem, San Francisco, Calif.

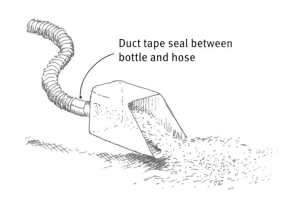

Duct tape seal between bottle and hose

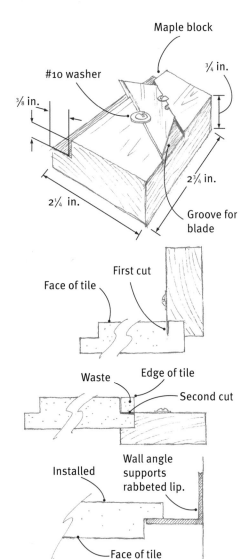

Maple block

#10 washer

3/8 in.

3/4 in.

2 3/4 in.

2 1/4 in.

Groove for blade

First cut

Face of tile

Waste

Edge of tile

Second cut

Installed

Wall angle supports rabbeted lip.

Face of tile

Rabbeting Ceiling Tiles

I INSTALL SUSPENDED CEILINGS FROM TIME TO TIME. So I made the tool shown in the drawing at left to help me rabbet the edges of the trimmed tiles. It's made of a maple block with a shallow groove for a utility-knife blade. The blade is held fast by a couple of screws.

To use the tool, I first pass it along the face of the tile, just scoring it. Then I make a second pass with the cutter at full depth. Another pass along its edge, and the tile is ready to drop in place.

—Jeff Bergstresser, Penn Yan, N.Y.

5

Masonry &
Foundation Work

Brick Cutter

THE DEVICE SHOWN IN THE DRAWING AT RIGHT is a simple but effective brick cutter that works by shearing a brick between a fixed angle iron and a brick chisel. It's not as fast as breaking bricks with a mason's hammer, but there will be more accurate cuts and a lot less waste. To make the cutter, file a true edge on the outside corner of a short piece of angle iron and place it on a heavy base, such as a beam off-cut, with the outside corner facing up. Secure the angle by placing the mitered end of a 2x4 tight against each side.

On one side of the angle, position a 1x6 up on a thick block to act as a guide for the brick chisel. Be sure to set the guide high enough to clear the thickest brick you plan to cut. Adjust its length so that when the bevel side of the brick chisel is held tight against the guide, the point of the chisel is directly over the edge of the angle iron. On the opposite side of the angle, place a support block to cradle the brick.

To use the cutter, place the brick on top of the angle with your mark centered over its edge. Position the chisel on top of the brick, bevel side tight against the guide. One or two blows with a heavy hammer should do the job. For face brick, cut the brick ⅛ in. to the waste side of the mark and clean up the exposed edge with short, controlled paring strokes of the chisel.

—Will Foster,
Aberdeen, Wash.

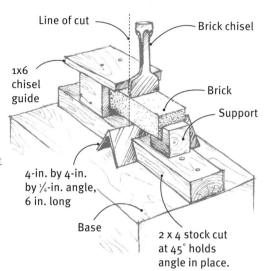

Anchoring to Concrete

ANCHORING WROUGHT IRON RAILINGS to concrete porches and stucco or concrete block walls can be a real problem. Pourable expansion cement offers a simple, reliable solution. It sets to usable hardness in half an hour and has twice the compressive strength of ordinary concrete. Expansion cement comes in powder form and can be mixed either to the consistency of putty for vertical work, or to pouring consistency for work on horizontal surfaces.

If you are working in old concrete, use a masonry drill or roto-hammer bit ½ in. larger than the diameter or diagonal measurement of the post to be installed, and drill a hole at least 2 in. deep. Rock and rotate the drill slightly to enlarge the bottom of the hole, then clean it out thoroughly, using an air compressor, bicycle pump, or vacuum cleaner. Dampen the hole with water, set the post in place, and fill it with expansion cement.

—Geoff Alexander, Berkeley, Calif.

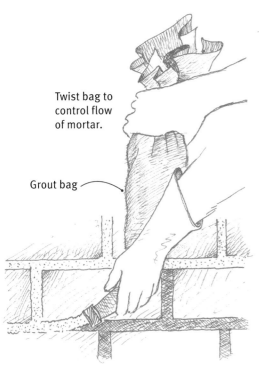

Twist bag to control flow of mortar.

Grout bag

Tuck Pointing

NOTHING WILL EVER MAKE REPOINTING old masonry a pleasure, but there is a tool that will take some of the drudgery out of it. Clean and prepare your joint lines as you usually do, then go out and buy a grout bag at a masonry supply store. I like the 24-in. model, but the size you'll wind up with usually depends on how strong you are—the bag gets heavy fast.

To use the bag, load in a mortar mix with just a touch more liquid than you normally use. Twist the open end of the bag or make a 90° fold in it to keep the mortar from oozing out the wrong way. Now position the nozzle so that the stream of mortar flows into your joint lines, as shown in the drawing at left. Wear rubber gloves during this operation, or plan on keeping the outside of the bag dry as a bone. If you don't you'll wind up with peeling skin on both hands. Once you've got the joint lines loaded with mortar, go back and compact them with your striking tool.

—John Dobrin, Washington, D.C.

Cone-Head Piers

WHEN I BUILD AN ARBOR, I like to elevate the posts above grade on concrete piers. The posts last longer that way, and if they ever need replacing, they are easy to remove. Usually I make individual tapered forms for each pier, but this time I decided to try something different: plastic 2-gal. plant containers.

As shown in the drawings below and at right, I cut the bottoms off the containers and then inverted them over a pad of freshly poured concrete. Once the concrete set, it was a snap to pull the forms off. They stack neatly in the shed, so now I've got eight forms on hand for the next job. The resulting cone shape makes a neat-looking detail and is strong.

—Dan Jensen, Tigard, Ore.

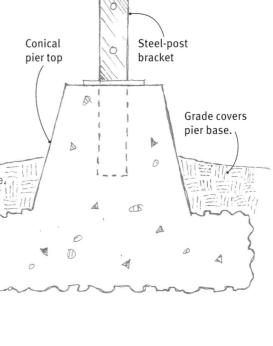

Conical pier top

Steel-post bracket

Grade covers pier base.

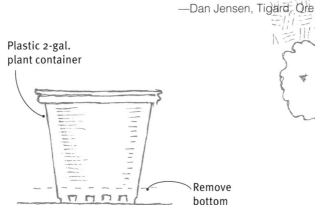

Plastic 2-gal. plant container

Remove bottom

PVC-Clad Piers

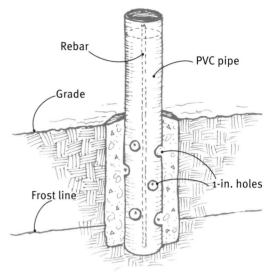

THE DRAWING AT RIGHT SHOWS MY PIER DESIGN for supporting decks and small buildings. The key to the system is the section of PVC drainpipe, which acts as both form and finish surface. I like the piers produced with this method because they are strong, cheap, easy to install, rustproof, rotproof, and good-looking.

I begin a pier by digging a 6-in.-to 8-in.-dia. hole with a post-hole auger to the required depth below the frost line. Next I use an electric drill with a wood-boring bit to punch several holes in a length of 4-in.-dia. PVC pipe. The holes allow the concrete inside and outside the pipe to combine for strength. For heavy or high structures I use 6-in. pipe.

Then I set the PVC pipe in the hole, leaving it a few inches longer than the final cut-off height. I pour concrete into the hole to grade level, and into the pipe to the desired height—a foot or so above grade. Then I set ½-in. rebar into the center of the pipe. The rebar can be left long to act as a pin, or be pushed below the level of the concrete. A J-bolt, angle iron, or other anchoring device can be added as well. While the concrete is still wet, I plumb the pipe and let the pier set overnight.

I made a cut-off marking jig from a 4-in. plastic coupling by grinding off the interior ridge so that the complete coupling slides down over the pipe. I mark the pipe for finished height with a scribe held against the jig, and cut it off with a reciprocating saw. Finally, I fill the remaining section of pipe with concrete and trowel it flush with the top of the pipe.

—Robert A. Ritchie, Westerly, R.I.

Gypboard Concrete Forms

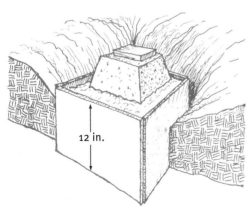

WE RECENTLY DID A FOUNDATION JOB in very crumbly, sandy soil. The first task was to set 27 pier blocks in pier holes that were 18 in. on a side and 12 in. deep. But by the time we had dug down a foot, we often had a hole that was more than 2 ft. across at the top and growing. Faced with filling these craters with concrete, we calculated that we would waste more than a cubic yard.

Instead of ordering the extra concrete, we transformed four sheets of gypboard into form boxes. We cut the sheets into 6-ft. lengths and scored them along their length at 18 in. o.c., leaving the face paper intact. Perpendicular to these scored lines, we cut the board into 12-in. wide strips. These strips were then folded into square boxes, placed in the oversized holes, and backfilled. The forms not only saved concrete, but also gave us an accurate way to calculate our ready-mix order.

—Sunrise Builders, Santa Cruz, Calif.

Standout Stakes

CONCRETE PATIOS, DRIVEWAYS, AND PATHS have to be sloped to promote good drainage, and I've poured more sloped concrete than I care to recall. The challenge with this kind of work is getting the levels right, and that means installing plenty of elevation stakes. But elevation stakes can be tough to drive into rocky soil or dry-clay soil. The stake ends up split or burred. And to make matters worse, wood stakes are easily lost in the excitement that often accompanies a concrete pour.

On my last sloped slab, I used stakes made of ½-in. copper water pipe. Not only were they easy to drive into the hard ground, but they were also equally easy to see as I raked the concrete and screeded it to its final elevation. Each pipe stood out as a perfect, dime-sized black spot against the light-gray concrete. Evidently the ½-in.-dia. hole is too small for the average piece of aggregate to clog, and the concrete cream doesn't have the viscosity necessary to span the hole. As soon as the concrete has been screeded to its final elevation, you can either pull out the stakes or drive them with a length of pipe beyond the bottom of the slab.

—Tony Toccalino, Milton, Ontario

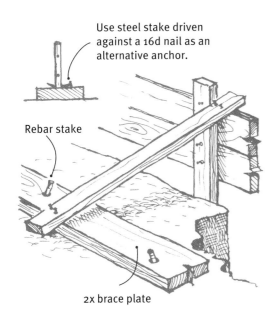

Use steel stake driven against a 16d nail as an alternative anchor.

Rebar stake

2x brace plate

Form Bracing in Loose Soil

IT CAN BE FRUSTRATING TO BRACE CONCRETE FORMS in loose soil—especially when the stakes begin to creep outward as the forms are filled. Faced with these soil conditions, I recently used a 2x brace plate to anchor my form braces.

As shown in the drawing at left, I positioned the plate far enough from my forms to give my braces about a 1:2 slope. The plate has 1-in. holes drilled 2 ft. on center. Through these holes I drove 2-ft. lengths of #4 rebar, oriented at opposing angles. Secured this way, the plate served as a sturdy anchor for my 2x4 braces.

If you get some steel stakes, use them to anchor the plate. As the end of the stake draws near to the plate, insert a 16d nail halfway through one of the holes and drive the stakes a little farther until the nail begins to bend as it engages the wood. When it comes time to remove the plates, lift them out of the ground with a backhoe. Lacking the backhoe, a pair of locking pliers makes a good handle on each stake.

—Michael Hermann, Nevada City, Calif.

Wire screen plugs gap
between form and trench.

Trench Plugs

I RECENTLY POURED GRADE BEAMS AND STEMWALLS for a house foundation on a hillside lot with stony soil. When the wooden form boards butted up to a trench or embankment, the irregular surface of the ground made for ragged gaps that were difficult to seal against the pressures of several feet of wet concrete.

To solve this problem, I used roofing nails to tack ¼-in. by ¼-in. wire screen over the ends of the form boards and across each gap, as shown in the drawing at left. The weight of the concrete forced the screen to sit tightly against the bumpy ground, and the screen kept the concrete inside the forms. In those places where the concrete pressure was greater or the gaps wider, I simply doubled up the wire.

—Glen Carlson, San Diego, Calif.

Homemade Rebar Bender

RECENTLY I WAS FORMING FOOTINGS for an addition and needed to rent a bender to put angles in the ½-in. rebar. It wasn't available at the local yard, so I improvised the simple tool shown in the drawing at right. It works well enough that, for me, renting rebar benders is a thing of the past.

My bender consists of two pieces of ¾-in. steel pipe—one 6 ft. long, the other 4 ft. long. In use, the 6-ft. length stays on the ground; the 4-ft. length is the lever. If I'm bending special pieces, I measure the rebar from end to bend, mark it, and slide the pipe over the rebar until the mark is between the two pipes. Lifting on the lever to the desired angle makes the bend.

For repetitive bends, I drilled a series of 3⁄16-in.-dia. holes, 6 in. apart, in the 6-ft. length of pipe. An 8d duplex nail in one of the holes serves as a stop.

—Dan Jensen, Tigard, Ore.

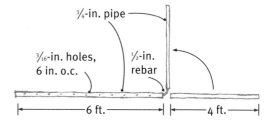

¾-in. pipe

3⁄16-in. holes, 6 in. o.c.

½-in. rebar

6 ft.

4 ft.

Giant-Contour Gauge

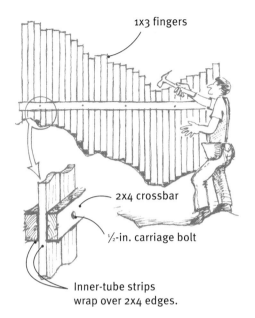

THE TOUGHEST PART ABOUT POURING A CONCRETE WALL atop a rocky ledge is getting the forms to match the undulating surface of the rocks. A bad fit under these circumstances can mean a lot of lost concrete and some heavy messes to clean up. Faced with this challenge, we took our inspiration from a tool usually put to use by trim carpenters—the contour gauge, as shown in the drawing at left.

Like the smaller version, ours had individual fingers held in place by a crossbar. The fingers can be moved independently to mimic an uneven surface. But instead of tiny stainless-steel pins, the fingers in our version are 1x3s. They are held in place by a pair of 2x4s, which are lined with inner tube to keep the fingers from easily slipping. Five ½-in. carriage bolts hold the thing together.

To use the gauge, we adjusted the 2x4 crossbar so that it was level, and then tapped the fingers down until they touched the ledge. When all the fingers were touching the ground, we tightened the bolts to make sure they wouldn't move. Then it was a simple matter to transfer the profile of the ground to our form plywood and cut out a perfect form—first time.

—Dan Tishman, Andy Williamson, Damariscotta, Maine

Image labels: 1x3 fingers; 2x4 crossbar; ½-in. carriage bolt; Inner-tube strips wrap over 2x4 edges.

Concrete Funnel

RECENTLY WE HAD TO FILL WITH CONCRETE the cells of some concrete-block piers. We naturally wanted the job to go quickly and neatly—no slopping wet concrete on the sides or at the base of the blocks. To help us with the pour, we used the plywood funnel shown in the drawing at right. It was held steady atop the blocks by the plywood ears extending into the block cells, and the curved cutouts allowed us to prop our buckets on the funnel edges without worrying about missing the mark.

—Gregory D. Lang, Cedar Key, Fla.

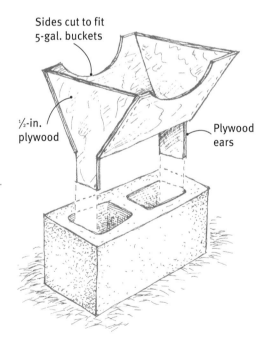

Image labels: Sides cut to fit 5-gal. buckets; ½-in. plywood; Plywood ears

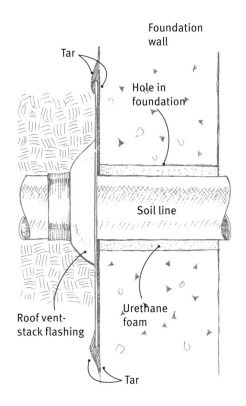

Foundation wall

Tar

Hole in foundation

Soil line

Roof vent-stack flashing

Urethane foam

Tar

Sealing a Drain Penetration in a Foundation Wall

LATELY, WE'VE BEEN SEARCHING for a better way to seal the gap around a drain pipe where it exits a foundation wall. The standard technique that most builders use in our area is to pack the gap with mortar or hydraulic cement. But lately, our plumbing inspectors have been frowning on this practice because any shift in the soil during frost cycles can crack a rigidly installed pipe. So we've tried a half-dozen different methods, with mixed results, until we started using the detail shown in the drawing at left.

Instead of mortar, we now use low-expansion urethane foam to fill the gap around the pipe. This is the same stuff we use to seal cracks and crevices throughout the house to reduce air leaks. Once the foam has cured, we apply a layer of roof cement to the outside of the wall. This is the thick stuff, the kind of roof cement that you spread with a trowel. Then we slip a roof vent-stack flashing over the pipe and bed the flashing in a ¼-in.-thick layer of roof tar. We lap the tar over the edges of the flashing to promote a better seal.

At backfill time, care must be taken to prevent damage to the flashing. This extra care has presented no problems for us, and we've had great luck with the results.

—Mike Guertin, East Greenwich, R.I.

Basement Wall Anchors

SOONER OR LATER A BASEMENT WALL ends up with a row of shelves on it, or buried behind layers of insulation and drywall. The nailing strips shown in the drawing at right will work to anchor these things and can be easily included in the basement walls as they are poured. I make a pair of nailers out of a single 2x6, ripped with beveled edges as shown in the detail. During the pour, I make sure to vibrate the concrete alongside the nailers to eliminate voids around their vertical edges.

Also, I don't bother with pressure-treated lumber for these nailers. If they stay dry, the nailers will last indefinitely. And a properly constructed basement wall is a dry wall.

—Burleigh F. Wyman, Whitefield, N.H.

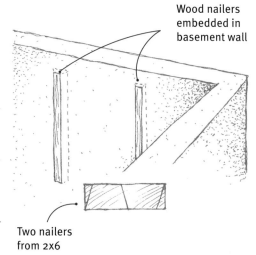

Wood nailers embedded in basement wall

Two nailers from 2x6

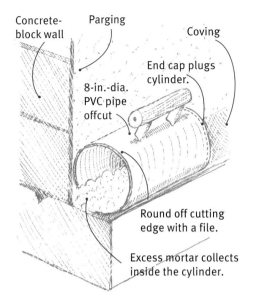

Concrete-block wall

Parging

Coving

End cap plugs cylinder.

8-in.-dia. PVC pipe offcut

Round off cutting edge with a file.

Excess mortar collects inside the cylinder.

Mortar-Coving Tool

HERE'S A SIMPLE WAY TO MAKE A NEAT JOB of the coving at the joint between a block wall and its footing. As shown in the drawing at left, I use a tool made from a length of 8-in. PVC pipe for this task. I salvaged the pipe from the scrap pile at my local plumbing supply, and while I was there, I bought an end cap, the kind that fits inside the pipe. To complete the tool, I mounted a handle on it and rounded the leading edge with a file.

To make the coved joint, I begin by piling mortar along the junction between the blocks and the footer. Then I use the tool in a back-and-forth screeding motion to pack the mortar into its coved shape. Excess mortar accumulates in the cylinder, to be reused farther down the foundation.

—James Elias, Orient, Ohio

Beveled Riser Forms

WHEN BUILDING FORMS FOR CONCRETE STEPS, use 2x material to form the risers as shown in the drawing at right, and cut a bevel along the bottom edge. This allows room for the finishing tools, such as the float and trowel, to reach to the back of the tread without having to wait for the forms to be stripped. The result is a tread with a uniform finish from the nosing to the riser.

—Walter H. Chandler, Richmond, Va.

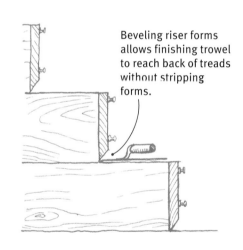

Beveling riser forms allows finishing trowel to reach back of treads without stripping forms.

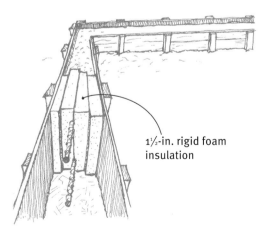

1½-in. rigid foam insulation

Form Stops

You can't always avoid cold joints in concrete, particularly in renovation work where things have to proceed incrementally. Here's an easy way to make a quick dam in your forms, even in places with lousy access.

Wedge pieces of 1½-in. rigid insulation into the forms like a row of books, as shown in the drawing at left. It's easy to cut channels in the foam for the protruding rebar, and the pieces will come out fairy easily once the pour has set up. Make sure to stagger the edges of the foam pieces to form a keyway for the next pour.

—Jim Ramsay, Kelownia, British Columbia

Anchor-Bolt Spacers

WHENEVER I BUILD FORMS FOR STEMWALL FOUNDATIONS, I like to have all my anchor bolts in place before the pour. This ensures proper alignment in the center of the mudsill, correct elevation (no chiseling the mudsill to accommodate the washer and nut), and accurate spacing so as not to interfere with my joist layout. In addition, this method guarantees a good bond between the concrete and the bolt and eliminates the problem of having to poke anchor bolts into concrete that has already begun to set up.

To position the bolts, I use 2-in. by 11-in. rippings of ⅝-in. or ¾-in. plywood. As shown in the drawing at right, the rippings also act as ties between opposing 2x form boards, and they can be reused many times. I drill holes in the ties to accept ½-in. anchor bolts. The holes are centered 4¼ in. from the outside end of the ties, with a bolt placed squarely in the middle of a 2x6 mudsill on an 8-in. stemwall. The bolts can be inserted through the holes with the nuts already on.

I typically tie each anchor bolt to the rebar to make sure the bolt stays put during a pour. Another way to keep the bolt in place as the concrete is poured around it is to slip a length of ¾-in. pipe over the bolt threads. This also keeps the concrete off the threads.

Here in California we have to install beefy hold-downs connected to large-diameter foundation bolts to keep buildings together during earthquakes. The bolts often have to be held exact distances above the finished stemwall. I use the plywood strips in conjunction with PVC pipe spacers (as shown in the detail drawing at right) to make sure the top of the bolt ends up just where I want it.

—Yon Mathiesen, Soquel, Calif.

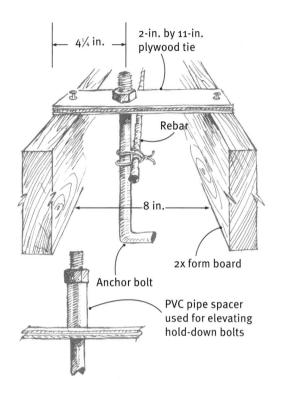

4¼ in.

2-in. by 11-in. plywood tie

Rebar

8 in.

2x form board

Anchor bolt

PVC pipe spacer used for elevating hold-down bolts

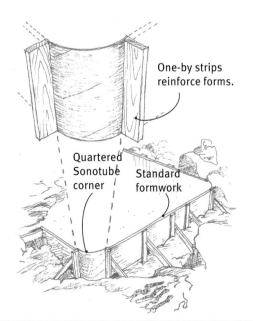

One-by strips reinforce forms.

Quartered Sonotube corner

Standard formwork

Round Corners for Concrete Forms

I WAS ON A JOB THAT REQUIRED a poured-concrete step with 6-in. radius curved corners. I've had good luck in the past using hardboard to form odd-shaped curves, but the material I had on hand wouldn't bend to this tight a radius. So I used sections of 12-in.-dia. Sonotube instead.

As shown in the drawing at left, I cut the tube to the correct length and then cut it into quarters lengthwise. Next, I affixed a couple of pieces of 1x furring strip to the outside edges of the forms, which provided me with the nailing flanges necessary to affix the tube sections to my forms.

—Robert V. Harrington, Milford, Conn.

6

Framing Solutions & Shortcuts

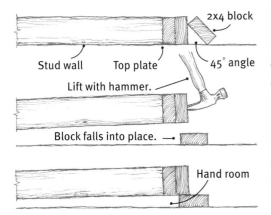

2x4 block

Stud wall   Top plate   45° angle

Lift with hammer.

Block falls into place. →

Hand room

Hand Room

BACK WHEN I WORKED IN THE TRACKS, a little trick made our lives easier when it came time to lift stud walls into place. Both people working on a wall would pick up a scrap piece of 2x4 and lean it against the top plate at about a 45° angle. Then we would bury the claw end of our hammers into the top plate deep enough to provide lifting purchase on the wall. Both workers lifting together would then raise the entire wall enough to allow the 2x4 blocks to fall under the top plate, providing hand room for the final lift from the other side.

—Dave Bullen, Berkeley, Calif.

Solo Framing

A CARPENTER WORKING ALONE can hold a header, blocking, or similar framing member in place for final nailing with a few bent nails. I use 8d nails, driven about a third of their length into the top edge of the work and then bent 90°. These ears will support the piece until the first nail is set.

—Craig Savage, Hope, Idaho

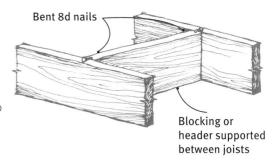

Bent 8d nails

Blocking or header supported between joists

Sheathing Cutouts

CARPENTERS OFTEN CUT OUT THE PLYWOOD SHEATHING from door and window openings with a reciprocating saw, circular saw, or even a chainsaw. I prefer to use a carbide-tipped pilot bit mounted in my router. This type of bit has a point on its tip, so it can be plunged into the center of the work. Above the tip is a pilot bearing, which will follow the framing as the cutters make a quick, clean cut in the sheathing.

—Michael Gornik, Nevada City, Calif.

A Strapping Idea

THE EASIEST WAY TO KEEP THE BOTTOM PLATE of a framed wall from walking when it is being raised is to toenail it into the subfloor. The nails bend easily as you lift the wall, and the bottom plate usually remains in the immediate neighborhood of its intended layout.

A more secure system uses the strapping that binds lumber loads. Cut it into 12-in. pieces and nail one end to the underside of the bottom plate. The other end should run under the wall and be nailed into the subfloor. Concrete nails will pierce the stuff, or you can abuse your ²⁄₃₂ nail set and start a hole. The strapping can be left in place and covered by the finish flooring.

—M.F. Marti, Monroe, Ore.

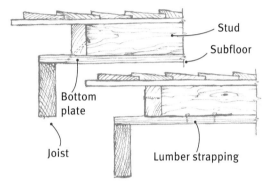

Stud

Subfloor

Bottom plate

Joist

Lumber strapping

Double-Beveled Rafters

CARPENTERS IN CENTRAL CALIFORNIA use this technique for cutting double bevels on hip or valley rafters fashioned from conventional 2x framing lumber. Set the tongue of the framing square on one end of the rafter as shown and draw two parallel pitch lines (they will be 1½ in. apart). Then adjust the foot of the circular saw to cut a 45° bevel, and make the first cut in the direction indicated in the drawing at right. The second cut starts from the opposite side of the board. The resulting double bevel allows the carpenter to tuck the rafter between two perpendicular common rafters.

—Andrew Kujawa, Santa Cruz, Calif.

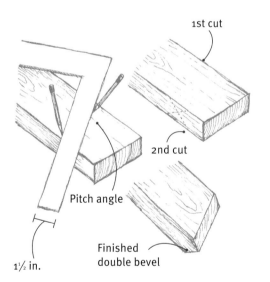

1st cut

2nd cut

Pitch angle

Finished double bevel

1½ in.

Courtesy Cuts

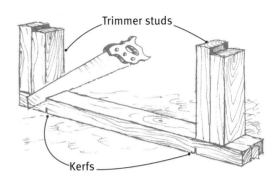

Trimmer studs

Kerfs

When I build stick-framed walls, I precut a portion of the sole plate where it has to be removed for doorways. I use my skillsaw to make kerfs about ¾-in. deep on the underside of the plate in line with the trimmer studs, as shown in the drawing. On long or heavy wall sections, I limit the kerf depth to about ½ in.

After the wall is assembled and erected, it's a simple matter to handsaw out the plate. This method saves time and the teeth on my favorite handsaw when I'm building on concrete floors, and still keeps the framing properly spaced and rigid as it's being raised.

—Brian P. Mitchell, Somerset, Colo.

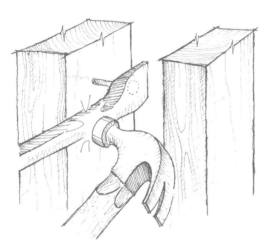

Tight-Spot Nailing

The next time you have to sink a nail in a place beyond your hammer's reach, try the technique shown in the drawing. Place the flat end of a 24-in. wrecking bar on the nail head, then hammer the bar shank a few inches from the nail. It works great in tight spots.

—Mike Lyon, Tacoma, Wash.

Plywood Protection

If your job-site plywood stack seems to be shrinking when you're not around, try screwing it down. I use 3-in. drywall screws to connect the top layers at the corners. The resulting 3-in.-thick plywood slab is heavy enough to discourage all but the most determined pilferers, and your plywood and whatever lies under it will stay put until needed.

—Michael R. Sweem, Downey, Calif.

45-Degree Corner Blocking

TO BLOCK 45-DEGREE CORNERS, I rip a 4x4 on the bandsaw, with the table set at 22.5. Then I use the ripped pieces at the ends of each wall section. This trick wastes no wood and also allows the sections to be securely nailed together.

—Ron Milner, Grass Valley, Calif.

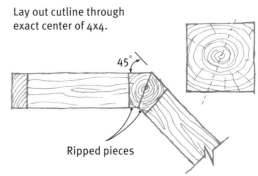

Lay out cutline through exact center of 4x4.

45°

Ripped pieces

Header Retrofit

TRY THIS TRICK NEXT TIME you put a built-up header into an existing wall. First, use a reciprocating saw to sever the nails at the top and bottom of all the studs to be removed. Now rotate the freed studs 90° and align them to one side of the bottom and top plates. Next, place trimmers (cut to their finished length) at an angle at either side of the opening. Raise one half of the header into place and tap the trimmers into their vertical position (depending on the span, a mid-support for the first half of the header may be required). Now you can remove the original studs and add the second half of the header. Spike the two halves together, and you're done.

—M. Felix Marti, Monroe, Ore.

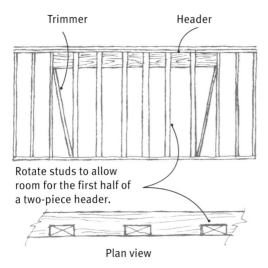

Trimmer   Header

Rotate studs to allow room for the first half of a two-piece header.

Plan view

Mudbucket Helpers

RECENTLY I CAME UP SHORTHANDED on a job site where we had planned to lay a ¾-in. T&G plywood deck. Knowing this can be a frustrating job even with help, I was loath to start it by myself. But there was no other work to do. Spying a trio of full joint-compound buckets, I decided to go ahead and put down some decking single-handedly. After nailing down the first row, I used the buckets as weights to hold down the tongues of the second row as I drove sheets home with a 2x4 and a sledge. This method worked so well that I got the entire deck laid before my tardy helpers arrived.

—Dennis Darrah, Montpelier, Vt.

Framing Under a Peak

PUTTING STUDS INTO THE WALL beneath the end rafters of a peaked roof can be time-consuming, but two simple jigs make it easy. Using a carpenter's square (or a calculator), determine the change in stud length (A in the bottom drawing at right). Assuming that the studs are equally spaced, this dimension is constant the entire length of the rafter. Now cut the ends of the studs at the angle that fits the rafter slope. Next, cut a piece of stud scrap to length A. The length of the shortest stud is found by measuring; from then on add the scrap block to the length of the previous stud and mark a cutting line, as shown in the top drawing at right.

Once cut, the studs will nail up easily if you make one more block. Cut another scrap piece as long as the distance between the stud faces (B in the bottom drawing at right) and use this as a spacer block. If you work accurately, the tops of the studs will wind up in the right position just by nailing.

—Kevin Kelly, Westfield, N.J.

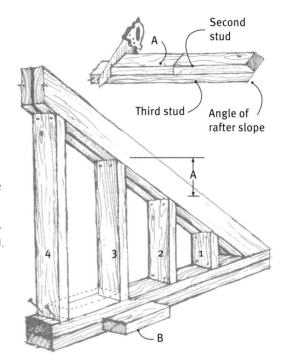

Second stud

A

Third stud

Angle of rafter slope

A

4   3   2   1

B

• •

Stud too close to allow hammer to swing

Slight bend angles nail toward target.

Intentionally Bent

HERE'S A SIMPLE AND EFFECTIVE WAY of nailing in tight places where your hammer is restricted, and the only angle of drive that you can use will result in the nail not catching both pieces of wood to be attached. Using your hammer, put a slight bend in the nail before driving it. Driven normally, the curvature of the nail will bring it right around into the required area as shown in the drawing at left. This method can make the last-minute installation of backing for bathroom fixtures, cabinets, or drywall almost bearable.

—Christopher Zane Nestor, Onalaska, Wis.

Strengthening Old Joists

ANYONE WHO HAS EVER RENOVATED AN OLD HOUSE has probably dealt with a floor system that is a bit too springy. It seems that 2x8 rough-cut joists were once used everywhere, regardless of the span.

I recently started work on a home built in the 1890s that has 2x8 joists on 16-in. centers, spanning 14 ft. They were also installed without blocking and were beginning to twist in spots. The basement has a dirt floor but plenty of headroom and usable floor space, so I didn't want to add a midspan beam with columns. Beefing up the joists was the only answer.

For blocking, I ran a 2x4 perpendicular to the joists across their bottoms at the center of the span. With the butt end of the 2x4 against the foundation, I worked my way across the floor, plumbing the joists and screwing through the 2x4 into each joist to secure them.

Next I turned each joist into a bowstring truss. I used drywall screws, steel straps, and construction adhesive to attach 2x4x12-ft. chords to the bottom of each joist, as shown in the drawing at right. I used five 3-in. drywall screws per side to pull the 2x4s into place over the block in the center of each joist. Then I added a pair of steel straps to get some fasteners working in shear in addition to withdrawal. This took only a few hours to do, and the floor now feels like it has 2x12 joists.

—David Wallace, Annapolis, Md.

Steel strap · Original 2x8 joist · 2x4x12-ft. chord · 2x4 run perpendicular to joists · 3-in. screws

More 45-Degree Corner Backing

I HAVE NOTICED THAT BACK ISSUES OF *FHB* have tips on stick-framed backing for 45° corners. While they're good methods, they require 4x4s and table saws, neither of which I usually have on-site.

To make corner backing out of 2x stock, I simply set my circular saw on 45° and remove one edge of a 2x4 stud. Then I nail the ripping onto the stud, filling the corner void as shown in the drawing at left. This method will also work with 2x6 studs if you make the rip ¾ in. from the corner instead of right on it. This method wastes no wood, requires no table saw and results in plenty of nailing surface.

—Tom Mahony, Kona, Hawaii

45° · 2x4 wall · 45° · 2x6 wall · ¾ in.

Wing-Wall Reinforcement

I WORKED ON A COMMERCIAL JOB last year where we had to build an office that included a 42-in.-tall, 5-ft.-long wing wall. The wall was built out of metal studs, covered with drywall, and finished along its top with a wood cap. The wall was held at one end by a bearing wall, but the only anchors holding the rest of the wall were the powder-actuated fasteners driven through the track into the slab. This had me worried. I was sure that, in time, people leaning on the wall would eventually weaken it to the point of collapse. So I strengthened the wall with concrete.

First I drilled a couple of ½-in.-dia. holes through the track and 6 in. into the slab for a pair of #4 rebar. As shown in the drawing at right, I placed them in the outermost bay of the wall. I used heavy-gauge steel studs for the two outer studs and turned them so that the flanges faced each other to lock into the concrete better. Then I screwed some scrap ⅝-in. plywood to the two studs, making a 3-ft.-tall form. Filled with concrete, the end of the wall became a cantilevered beam that is quite strong. The drywallers glued the drywall to the concrete, and we were done.

—Chris Sturm, Hamburg, Pa.

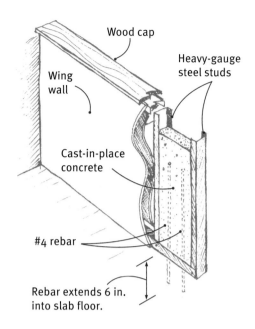

Wood cap

Heavy-gauge steel studs

Wing wall

Cast-in-place concrete

#4 rebar

Rebar extends 6 in. into slab floor.

Floor-Joist Reinforcement

I JUST REMODELED A KITCHEN, adding granite countertops, a heavy, commercial-style range, and ceramic-tile floors. I was concerned about the floor's flexibility. If it was too bouncy, the grout would eventually loosen and pop out.

There was a finished basement below the kitchen, so adding posts to bolster the floor wasn't an option. But the basement's suspended ceiling was easy to remove, which gave me access to the 2x10 joists under the kitchen floor.

As shown in the drawing at left, I used continuous steel wall-bracing straps as tension rods to stiffen each joist. I wrapped the joists from the top of one end, around the bottom at midpoint, and back to the top of the opposite end. I nailed the strap to the joist every few inches with joist-hanger nails. The floor was substantially stiffened by this procedure, and so far, the grout has remained intact.

—Tim Brigham, Koloa, Kauai, Hawaii

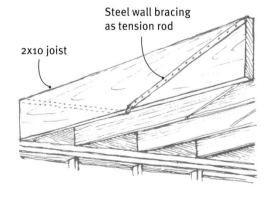

Steel wall bracing as tension rod

2x10 joist

Hard-to-Reach Nailing

WHEN I NEED TO SET A NAIL that is just out of reach of my hands but not my hammer, I lengthen my reach with a board with a small kerf in its end, as shown in the drawing at right. I wedge a nail into the kerf, and then hold the nail on the target until I can set the nail with a couple of hammer taps. This technique is safer than the contorted acrobatics that I've seen some carpenters resort to, and quicker than setting up a ladder.

—Rick Hatten, Bainbridge Island, Wash.

Kerf holds nail for hard-to-reach nail setting.

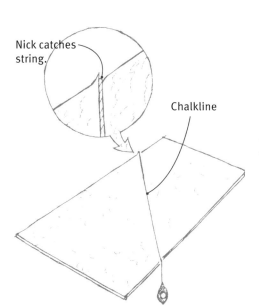

Nick catches string.

Chalkline

Snapping Diagonal Chalklines

IF YOU'VE EVER TRIED TO SNAP A DIAGONAL CHALKLINE across a piece of plywood, you know how frustrating it can be. Past a certain angle, the line's hook just won't hang on to the edge of the plywood. The drawing at left shows how I deal with the problem. I use a utility knife to make a small nick in the edge of the plywood. Then I slip the string into the resulting slot. Now the string hangs on while I snap my line.

—Phillip Carpendale, Nelson, British Columbia

Leveling an Old Ceiling

IF YOU HAVE EVER REHABBED AN OLDER BUILDING, you know about the problem of uneven ceilings. Once plaster and lath have been removed, there is often variation among ceiling joists, especially if the building has settled. These conditions make it frustrating to hang drywall and result in a job that doesn't look professional.

The method we use to level the ceiling field uses metal studs screwed to the sides of the old joists, as shown in the drawing at right. But before we start installing the studs, we first get on a ladder and determine the ceiling's lowest point. Then we make a mark on the wall about ½ in. below that point. Using a water level, we transfer this mark to all of the walls around the room. Then we connect the marks with a chalkline. This line marks the new level for the ceiling.

We screw the metal studs to the old joists with 1¼-in. drywall screws, 2 ft. o.c. If we have a long span, we simply piece together as many studs as necessary, aligning them with a stringline to make sure they stay straight. We like metal studs because they are relatively cheap and absolutely straight. We do, however, use wood blocking along the edges of the ceiling to reinforce the perimeter and to provide backing for crown molding.

—John Berglund, Tom Canning, St. Louis, Mo.

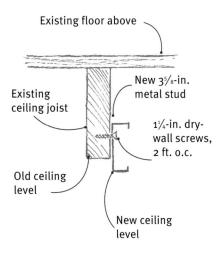

Existing floor above

Existing ceiling joist

New 3⅝-in. metal stud

1¼-in. drywall screws, 2 ft. o.c.

Old ceiling level

New ceiling level

Crown Your Studs

BUILDERS ROUTINELY CROWN THEIR RAFTERS and joists, but I don't know many who crown their studs as well. That's too bad because there are a couple of benefits. First, because each stud is looked at with a critical eye, the really bad ones are rejected for use in less critical places. Second, with all the crowns pointing in the same direction, you don't get a wave in the wall where studs with moderate crown alternate in and out. This condition is especially apparent on walls with chair rails or cabinets on the inside, and those with hardboard siding on the outside.

—Robert Countryman, Ranger, Ga.

Built-Up Beam

THE HOUSE I RECENTLY WORKED ON has a balcony that spans 23 ft. over the living room. The plans called for a 6-in. by 22-in. by 24-ft. beam to carry the balcony, but such a beam proved hard to find—even a laminated version. We considered using a steel I-beam, but the rough framing was nearly complete, and a soggy site suggested a difficult delivery. So builder Charlie Callahan and I worked out this simple site-built plywood box beam as an alternative.

First we set the balcony floor joists on a temporary partition on top of the joists, forming a balcony curb. Three 2x4s were spiked together under the joists for the bottom chord of the beam. Since our clear span was 23 ft. and we needed 6 in. of bearing at both ends, we cast about for 24-ft. framing lumber. We were fortunate to find some locally, so we didn't need to splice any chords. However, splices are permissible in this kind of beam if they are staggered, and glued as well as nailed.

To connect the top and bottom chords of the beam, we covered both sides with ½-in. plywood, nailed and glued. We used sheets 22½ in. by 8 ft. on the outside face of the beam. On the inside face, we covered the spaces between the joists with pieces that were 22½ in. square. The beam is wrapped with T&G oak as a finish.

This beam is exceptionally strong, and it acts as one with the balcony "joists to resist twisting. It was also fast and easy to build in place. We engineered the beam with the help of American Plywood Association's "Plywood Design Specification," Supplement #2. Single copies are available free from APA, 7011 S. 19th St., Tacoma, Wash., 98466.

—Frank Lee, Baltimore, Md.

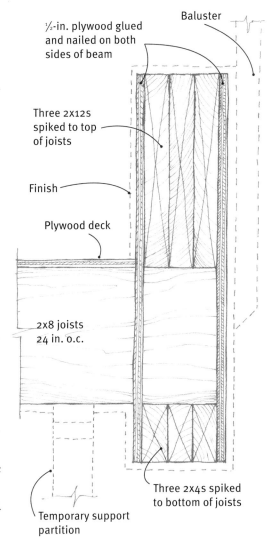

½-in. plywood glued and nailed on both sides of beam

Baluster

Three 2x12s spiked to top of joists

Finish

Plywood deck

2x8 joists 24 in. o.c.

Temporary support partition

Three 2x4s spiked to bottom of joists

Positioning Stud Walls

BEFORE I RAISE A STUD WALL, I find it helpful to toenail it with 16d nails onto the layout line as shown in the drawing at left. As the wall is hoisted into position, the nails act as a hinge as they bend. The wall ends up on the layout line with little need for adjustments and no protruding nails.

—Zack Mills, Olympia, Wash.

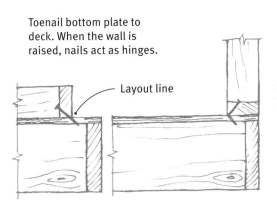

Toenail bottom plate to deck. When the wall is raised, nails act as hinges.

Layout line

Splicing Ridge Boards

As a framing carpenter, I frequently come across a ridge span longer than the overall length of the material I'm using for the ridge. To extend the material to the correct length, I splice ridge boards with a V-shaped joint as shown in the drawing at right.

My crew and I call this technique "penciling the ridges," after the big pencil-shaped piece of wood that results when the cuts are made. To begin the cuts, overlap the ridge material with the crowns pointing in the same direction. The overlap should be at least equal to the rafter spacing (usually 16 in. around here). Now take your tape and mark the rafter layout lines as shown in the drawing. Draw cutlines from the center of the top ridge board to its end, and make these cuts with the sawblade set ⅛ in. deeper than the cut. This will put saw tracks in the bottom piece, showing you where to finish the cuts.

Now you can put the pieces together with a couple of 8d nails near the end of the splice. Depending on how long the pieces are, you either can assemble them on the ground and carry them to the ridge or put them together in place.

I like this detail because it's clean and because it holds together better than a couple of toenailed, butt-joined boards. It's also simpler than scabbing on a plywood gusset or a 2x splice.

—Ryan Hawks, Flagstaff, Ariz.

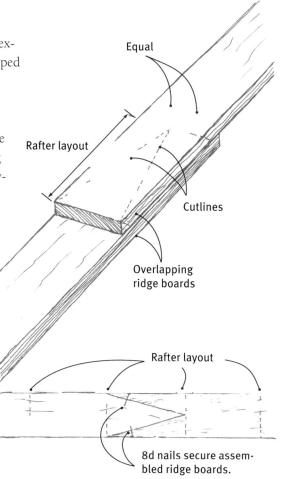

Equal

Rafter layout

Cutlines

Overlapping ridge boards

Rafter layout

8d nails secure assembled ridge boards.

No-Nail Zone

An old carpenter once advised me not to use nails in the area 12 in. to 24 in. above the sole (bottom) plate at places such as built-up corners, trimmers, or doubled studs. This way, holes for electrical wiring can be drilled at typical outlet heights without running into nails. It sure saves a lot of auger bits.

—Dick Haward, Nehalem, Ore.

Measuring Odd Shapes

ONE DAY WHEN I WAS TRYING TO FIGURE OUT how to cut an irregular six-sided piece of roof sheathing, another carpenter showed me a trick used by boat builders to mark the outline of oddball workpieces quickly. The method is called tick sticking. To do it, all you need is a scrap of plywood and a pointed stick.

As shown in the drawing at right, begin by affixing a plywood scrap to a point along the edge of the hole in need of sheathing. It's handy but not necessary for the scrap to be near a corner. It will give you a ready point of reference.

Now take the stick and lay it across the plywood scrap so that the point of the stick touches one of the corners of the hole. Draw a line along the edge of the stick, and then mark a "tick" on the stick and a corresponding tick on the plywood scrap. Mark them both #1. Do this for each corner, assigning each one numbers. I work from left to right as I make my marks, but you can use any order that suits you.

Once the marks have all been recorded, place the scrap of plywood next to the material you are going to cut and reverse the process. Lay the stick on the lines, align the ticks, and then note the positions of the corners. Connect the corner marks, and you've got the outline of the workpiece. This method is accurate, easy, cheap, and low-tech.

—Phillip Carpendale, Nelson, British Columbia

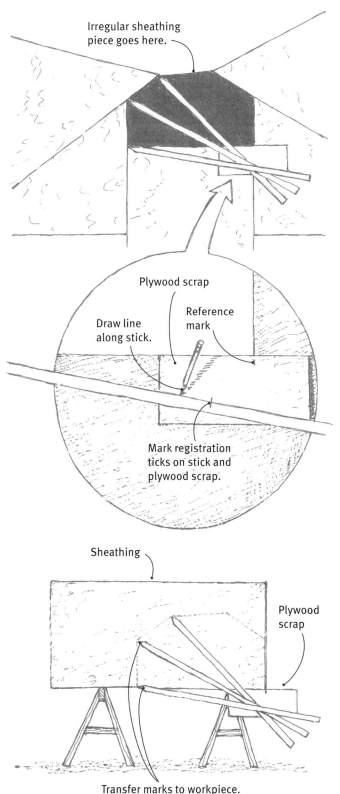

Irregular sheathing piece goes here.

Plywood scrap

Reference mark

Draw line along stick.

Mark registration ticks on stick and plywood scrap.

Sheathing

Plywood scrap

Transfer marks to workpiece.

7

Framing Jigs

Framing Jig

I HAVE A RAPID AND ACCURATE METHOD for assembling any wall, floor, or roof that uses standard dimensions. It consists of a jig, which is simply a 2x4 notched on 16-in. or 24-in. centerlines to receive the framing members. Two such jigs are handy, and for large-scale work, four can help. To use, just slip one member at a time into the jig until everything is in place, then nail. No measuring is required except for cutting pieces to length. It really helps on long runs that need to be sheetrocked, covered with plywood, etc. For trusses, it means that everything can get assembled via the jigs, the plywood started, and then the jigs pulled up. No nails to pull.

I put together a 1,000-sq.-ft. workshop with this method—mostly by myself and on evenings and weekends. It really works.

—M. R. Havens, St. Albans, W.Va.

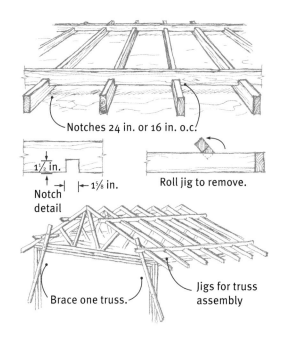

Notches 24 in. or 16 in. o.c.

1½ in.

1⅝ in.

Notch detail

Roll jig to remove.

Brace one truss.

Jigs for truss assembly

Straightening Warped Deck Boards

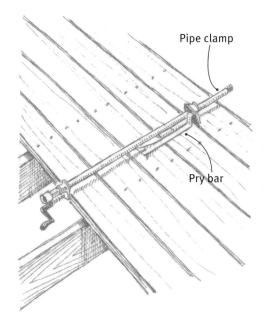

Pipe clamp

Pry bar

IF YOU BUILD DECKS, sooner or later you'll have to develop a method for straightening stubborn deck boards. After struggling with a number of techniques with varying degrees of success, I discovered one afternoon that I could combine two tools that I always have on-site to coax any board into place. As shown in the drawing at left, I placed the short end of a pry bar in the gap between two boards that had already been installed. The long end of the pry bar points toward the board you're installing. Then I placed the tail stop of the pipe clamp over the pry bar and the clamp's head on the workpiece. With a couple of turns of the crank, the deck board is ready to nail off. Too easy.

—Brian Simmons, Oakland, Calif.

The Hooter Stick

PLUMBING AND ALIGNING STUD WALLS can be quite a chore, some-times involving the better part of a five- or six-man crew. On a recent job, I became acquainted with the tool shown in the drawing at right. Here in Austin, Texas, it's called a hooter stick, and I haven't found anything that's better suited for adjusting long, tall, or just plain awkward walls.

Basically it is nothing more than two studs, a 2x4 block 20 in. to 30 in. long, and an old hinge. To assemble the stick, first cut a 45° V-notch in the end of one stud and scab the block flush to the bottom end of the other stud. Then fasten the two parts with the hinge.

To use the hooter stick, place the notched end against the underside of the top plate, near a corner or an intersection with another wall. To brace the bottom of the stick you can use either your foot or a block that is tacked to the subfloor. Now you're ready to push in the direction that you want the wall to move. The hooter is an awkward piece of equipment to manipulate at first, but once you get used to it you'll be surprised at what you can do to an outside wall full of offsets and headers.

—Paul Wilson, Austin, Tex.

2x4 studs · V-notch · Door hinge · 20-in. to 30-in. scab block

Hanging Fascia Boards

IT USUALLY TAKES TWO PEOPLE to hang fascia boards. Even then it can be pretty precarious out there on the end of a rafter, straining to support a heavy fascia board with one hand while trying to line up a mitered corner and sink a galvanized 16d nail with the other hand. With the help of the simple jig in the drawing at left, even one person can do it.

I tack one jig near each end of the fascia. I drive the nails just far enough to support the weight of the fascia. Then I lower the fascia into the slots in the jigs (the slots should be a little oversize to prevent binding). The jigs hold the fascia in approximately the right place while I adjust it for alignment and nail it into place.

—Neal Bahrman, Ventura, Calif.

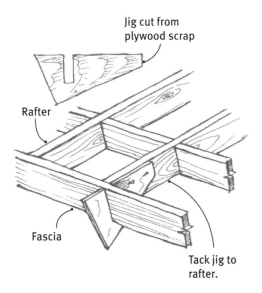

Jig cut from plywood scrap · Rafter · Fascia · Tack jig to rafter.

Block-Cutting Guide

THE HOMEMADE DEVICE shown below is one of those gadgets that makes me wonder the proverbial "Why didn't I think of that?" Designed by Andrew Kerley, the tool is a triangle made of ½-in. plywood. As shown in the top portion of the drawing, the body of the guide is a right triangle with truncated tips. The length of the triangle's legs is equal to the length of the block you want to cut, minus 1½ in. As shown in the bottom portion of the drawing, the 1½ in. in. takes into account the distance from the base of a typical worm-drive saw to its blade. The guide shown here is designed to cut blocks that are 14½ in. long in one position. Flip it over, and it guides the saw through a 13-in. block. You can modify the dimensions to cut blocks of any length and to accommodate the different blade offset of a sidewinder saw.

Note that the fences each have a hook on one end. To use the guide, lay it on the material to be cut, and snug the hook to the end of the stock. Run the saw along the guide and repeat as necessary. If you need to take a little off the length of the block, put a thumbtack on the hook.

—Larry Haun, Coos Bay, Ore.

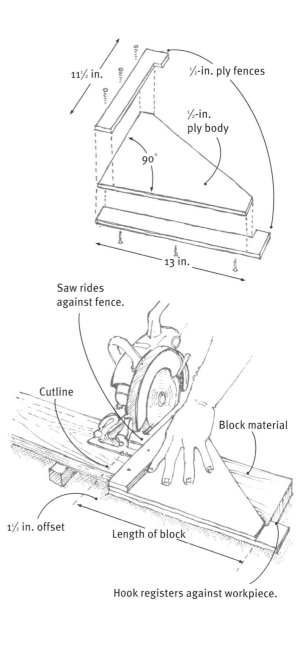

11½ in.

½-in. ply fences

½-in. ply body

90°

13 in.

Saw rides against fence.

Cutline

Block material

1½ in. offset

Length of block

Hook registers against workpiece.

Decking Persuader

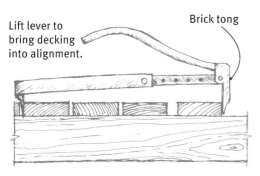

Lift lever to bring decking into alignment.

Brick tong

I USE A BRICK TONG TO ALIGN DECKING BOARDS. The stationary end of the tong can be wedged between two nailed deck boards, and the pivoting end can be used to bring a board in, or, if the anchoring end is moved back one board width, to push it out. Either way the action is fast and simple. Because you need one hand to hold the tong handle, it helps to start the nail before pulling on the board. You may also want to drill a couple of new holes in the tong's adjustment bar to get the spacing right.

—Phil Cyr, Dudley, Mass.

Wall-Lift Prop Poles

WITH THREE OR FOUR OF THE SITE-BUILT WALL JACKS shown in the drawing at right, a two-man crew can lift 30-ft.- to 40-ft.-long stud walls. Each jack is made of a 2x4 about 7 ft. long with three nailed-on scabs, 2 ft. apart. The scabs form ledges to support the wall as it is lifted.

With the stud wall lying flat on the subfloor and toenailed to it, toenail each jack to the floor so that its base is tight to the wall's top plate. Now begin at one end of the wall and lift it to the first notch. Move back and forth along the wall, lifting one notch at each station until you've reached the third level. From there it's an easy push to get the wall upright.

—Ed Wilson, Seattle, Wash.

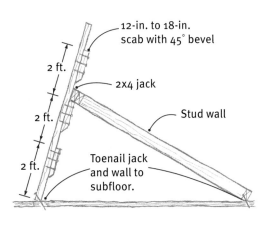

12-in. to 18-in. scab with 45° bevel

2 ft.

2x4 jack

Stud wall

2 ft.

2 ft.

Toenail jack and wall to subfloor.

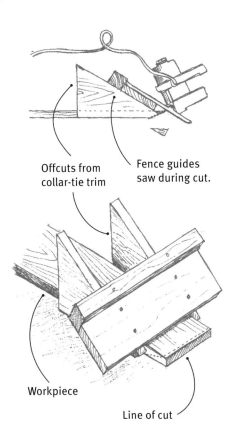

Offcuts from collar-tie trim

Fence guides saw during cut.

Workpiece

Line of cut

Acute-Angle Cut-Off Fixture

I HAD A JOB BOXING SOME COLLAR TIES with 1x trim boards, and the bevel cut was beyond the reach of my circular saw. The 7-in-12 pitch of the roof meant that I needed a 30° angle on the ends of the boards that trimmed the tops and bottoms of the collar ties. Making that cut would require my circular saw to lean over at a 60° angle, 15° past its maximum. Solving the problem led me to devise the cut-off fixture shown in the drawing at left. First I linked a couple of the offcuts from the 1xs that trim the sides of the collar ties with a piece of wood that serves as a bed for the saw to ride on. A fence affixed to the upper edge of this bed guides the saw's foot.

To make the bevel cuts, I placed a length of stock in the fixture, set the saw to make a 30° cut, and ran the saw over the workpiece as shown in the top portion of the drawing. Result: a clean 30° bevel. By the way, if the blade doesn't reach deep enough to cut all the way through the stock with a single pass, use a handsaw to finish the cut.

—Brian Martin, Grottoes, Va.

Homemade Water Level

LET'S SAY YOU'VE JUST PUT FOUR POSTS IN THE GROUND for a sun deck and now need to cut them all off at the same height. What do you do? If you have a builder's level or transit you're all set, but if you don't, this water level is a very simple and inexpensive way to solve the problem. It consists of any length of clear plastic tubing (or a hose with clear plastic extensions at the end) and works on the principle that water seeks its own level.

First, fill the tubing with water, leaving a foot or two of air at the ends, and hold one end against the point to be transferred, as shown in the drawing at right. Another worker takes the other end of the tubing to the first post to be cut off (post B in the drawing).

The person at post B holds the tubing against it while the person at the other end moves the tubing up or down until the water level in the tubing matches the level of the point to be transferred. When this has been accomplished, the water line in the tubing at post B will be the same as at the transfer point.

Always transfer levels from the original point to lessen accumulated error. Remove all the air bubbles from the tubing—they can affect accuracy. Remember that no part of the tubing should be higher than the ends.

This tool is useful in many ways on a building site. We use it whenever we need to transfer a level point farther than the length of a carpenter's level.

—David Barker, Gardiner, Maine

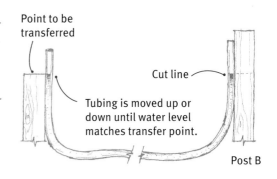

Point to be transferred

Cut line

Tubing is moved up or down until water level matches transfer point.

Post B

Picket Gauge Stick

THE NEXT TIME YOU'RE ASSEMBLING RAILING PICKETS on a deck, try using a gauge stick to speed assembly. As shown in the drawing at left, the gauge stick fits between pickets. Spacers at its top and bottom make it easy to align the next picket, while the gauge stick's foot rests on the decking.

—Louis J. Fritz, Medford Lakes, N.J.

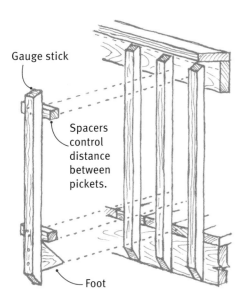

Gauge stick

Spacers control distance between pickets.

Foot

Subfloor Sheathing Persuader

LAYING TONGUE-AND-GROOVE SUBFLOOR SHEATHING usually calls for at least two carpenters. As one wields a sledgehammer on the sheet to be threaded, the other is easing the tongue of this sheet into the groove of the sheets in the preceding course by shifting weight from foot to foot.

The large T-square shown at right can eliminate one of these jobs. It uses a 2x6 about 4 ft. long as a crossbar, and a 2x4 handle about 5 ft. long. With the subfloor panel in position, run the crossbar out on the joist tops with the handle held only 12 in. off the deck. Then pull it back with a lot of force against the grooved side of the panel while keeping the balls of your feet on the seam to be threaded.

—Malcolm McDaniel, Berkeley, Calif.

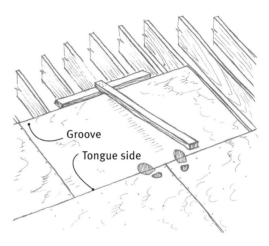

Groove

Tongue side

The Twister

ONE OF THE FIRST THINGS WE DO on a new framing site is to build a "twister" to help straighten corkscrewed lumber. Our twisters are made of two 3-ft. 2x4s and one 2-ft. 2x4. As shown in the drawing at left, the long 2x4s sandwich the short one, creating a slot at one end. To use the twister, we nail the twisted piece of stock at one end. Then we slip the tool over the other end and move the twister until the stock comes flush with its nailing surface. The twister usually provides enough leverage that it only takes one hand, leaving the other free to swing a hammer or fire a nailer.

—Sean Sheehan, Basin, Mont.

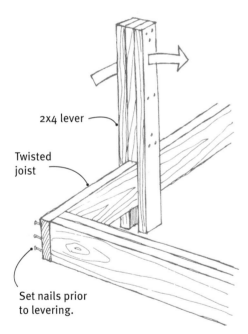

2x4 lever

Twisted joist

Set nails prior to levering.

The Glue Sled

CALL ME PERSNICKETY, but I like to place a nice full bead of construction adhesive down the center of the floor joists before I lay down a sheet of plywood subflooring. Too many times, I've been on a job site where the glue was applied carelessly, resulting in an erratic line with skips and unacceptably thin smears. If it's worth the expense and effort of gluing a subfloor in the first place (and I think it is), then it's worth taking the time to do it right. The device shown at right is my solution to the problem. I think the best part is that using this gadget, I center the glue bead on the joist every time without having to go back.

The glue sled, as I call it, is nothing more than a 1⅝-in.-wide block of ¾-in. pine with a hole in it. The block is sandwiched between ¼-in.-thick plywood sides. The hole accepts the nozzle of the glue cartridge, and the rubber band loops over the caulk-gun frame, holding the sled in place. In use, the plywood sides ride along the sides of the joist, keeping the nozzle centered.

I think a ³⁄₁₆-dia. bead of glue is the ideal amount. And although I don't obsess over this detail, I can tell you that cutting the nozzle ⅜ in. from its tip yields a ³⁄₁₆-in. opening for the glue to exit. If your joists are on 16-in. centers, figure on using about three-quarters of a 10.5-oz. tube per sheet of plywood. Where sheets come together on one joist, you can get a fairly even off-center bead of glue by lifting up the sled and angling the glue gun to the side.

—Herrick Kimball, Moravia, N.Y.

⅝-in. hole for nozzle

Rubber band

¾-in. pine body

Rubber band hooks over frame.

¼-in. plywood sides

1⅝ in.

Glue sled

Glue sled in use (side removed for clarity)

Joist

8

Roofing, Siding & Exterior Trim

Shingle Shelf

WHEN WOOD SHINGLING A ROOF or sidewall, keeping a ready supply of shingles close at hand can be a problem. The simple shelf shown in the drawing at right can be secured by tucking the tapered tab under an already-nailed course of shingles. In this way, shingles can be kept conveniently close to the height at which you are working, instead of down by your feet on the staging. A bunch of these shelves can be made from rejected shingles and scraps of 1x6s or 1x8s. Cutting the top corners off the shingle part of the shelf makes it easy to slip it up under a course.

—Kendall Gifford, Putney, Vt.

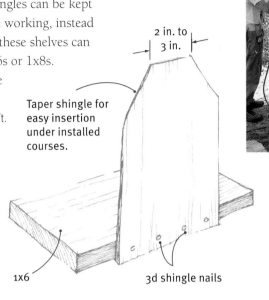

2 in. to 3 in.

Taper shingle for easy insertion under installed courses.

1x6

3d shingle nails

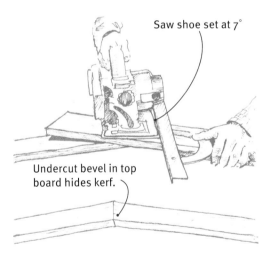

Saw shoe set at 7°

Undercut bevel in top board hides kerf.

Double Cuts

HERE'S A QUICK WAY TO GET A TIGHT JOINT with ¾-in.-thick rake boards where they meet at the roof peak. Tack your two rake boards in place on the gable end, letting them run wild at the top, one over the other, to form an X. Mark your plumb cut. Set the proper depth on your saw and your shoe angle at 7° and cut through both boards at the same time. You want the bevel in the top board to be an undercut, as shown, so lap the boards accordingly. This will be a function of which way the shoe on your saw tilts, and whether you are cutting from above on the ridge or from below on a scaffold or ladder. This trick also works on straight cuts to join long runs of fascia.

—Matthew Giordano, Plymouth, Mich.

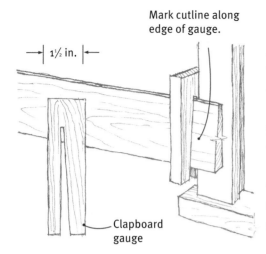

Mark cutline along
edge of gauge.

1½ in.

Clapboard
gauge

Clapboard Gauge

THE MARKING DEVICE shown in the drawing at left is used to establish cutlines for clapboards where they abut trim pieces. I find it to be especially handy for recladding old houses where the casings and cornerboards aren't plumb.

I make the gauge from a scrap of ¾-in.-thick pine, 1½ in. wide. The slot in the center of the gauge should fit the profile of your clapboards just tightly enough to hold a clapboard in place.

To use the gauge, hold your clapboard with the end to be cut running by the casing and slip the gauge over the clapboard. Press the gauge tightly against the casing and scribe along the edge of the gauge. Cut along the line, and the clapboard will fit tightly against the trim board.

—Duke York, Willimantic, Conn.

Cutting Clapboards

WHEN REMODELING OR BUILDING ADDITIONS, it is often necessary to cut existing clapboard siding along a vertical line. Problem is, the saw's shoe wants to hang up on the protruding lower edges of the clapboards, which in turn makes the blade dip into the sheathing underneath it. To ensure a cut of even depth, I tack a ¾-in.-thick base strip to the siding, as shown in the drawing at right. Then I set the saw to cut a depth equal to the thickness of the base strip plus that of the siding. As the saw's foot rides on the base strip during the cut, a constant depth is maintained. To make the cut even more accurate, you can tack a guide for the side of the saw's shoe to the base strip.

—Loran Smith, Dover, N.H.

Saw rides on
base strip.

Cutting Asphalt Shingles

IT'S A MESSY JOB, but sometimes I have to plunge my circular saw through several layers of asphalt shingles to cut a hole in an old roof. Before I bury my carbide-tipped sawblade in the shingles, I give it a good dose of Pledge spray wax. The wax keeps the tar in the shingles from adhering to the blade or to the saw's discharge chute. Reapplications of the wax are necessary, but the roofing cuts like wood.

—James Blohm, Amityville, N.Y.

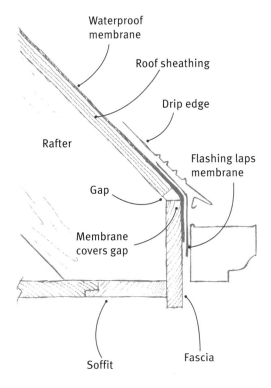

Waterproof membrane

Roof sheathing

Drip edge

Rafter

Flashing laps membrane

Gap

Membrane covers gap

Soffit

Fascia

Ice-Dam Advice

THE WINTER OF 1993–94 WAS TOUGH on buildings in the Northeast. Many houses and commercial buildings around here experienced damage from ice dams for the first time. In the course of repairing a number of houses, I repeatedly found that the roofing installers had not sealed a common route that ice follows into a roof: the gap between the fascia and the roof sheathing.

What I found in roof after roof that had gutters was that ice and water would go under the drip edge and get into the roof through that gap. These roofs also had 3-ft.-wide self-adhering waterproof membranes along the eaves, membranes that are supposed to shield the structure from ice and water damage.

The drawing at left shows how I've modified the typical roof-edge detail to correct the problem that resulted from the gap. I run the waterproof membrane a couple of inches down the fascia to a point below the level of the gutters. Because waterproof membranes aren't rated for exposure to sunlight, I cover the membrane with a piece of flashing that runs from the edge of the roof sheathing to the middle of the fascia. With this detail, ice buildups forming up from the gutter might get under the drip edge, but they can't get through the gap.

—Chuck Green, Ashland, Mass.

Siding Holdup

ONE NIGHT I WENT TO BED DREADING THE NEXT DAY. Working solo, I'd be siding the gable end of a house with clapboards, my only helper on the ground cutting and handing me the material. Like magic, the solution to my problem came to me in a dream that night.

As shown in the drawing at right, I made an S-shaped clip out of a 4-in.-sq. piece of sheet metal. In use, the top leg of the clip hangs over the prior course of siding, while the bottom leg supports the next course. The arrangement allowed me to get a few nails into each course to keep it aligned before pulling the clip out and moving it up. My "Trip Clip" also proved to be handy for supporting the end of my tape measure over long runs.

—Trip Renn, Chapel Hill, N.C.

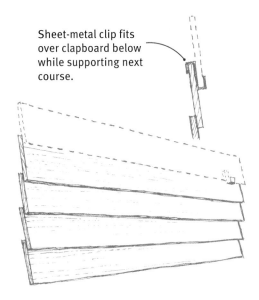

Sheet-metal clip fits over clapboard below while supporting next course.

Marking a Square Cut on a Round Column

RECENTLY, I HAD TO CUT AN 8-IN.-DIA. WOOD COLUMN to length. The trick was to make sure the round column was cut exactly square. Because it was too big for my miter box, I started mulling over my options. Then a colleague recommended a simple solution. All it required was a length of paper with a straight edge long enough to wrap around the circumference of the column.

As shown in the drawing at right, I used a piece of rosin paper to encircle the column at the required length. When the edge of the paper was aligned, I marked my cut and used a jigsaw to lop off the unwanted portion of the column. Note in the section of the column how I angled the jigsaw a bit to create a slight back cut to ensure a tight fit where the column sits on its base.

—Patrick A. Molzahn, Oregon, Wis.

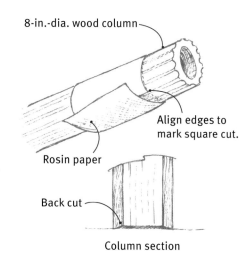

8-in.-dia. wood column

Align edges to mark square cut.

Rosin paper

Back cut

Column section

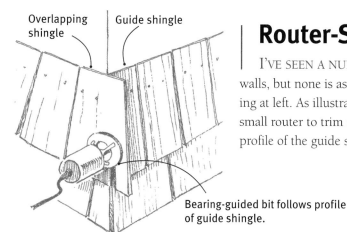

Overlapping shingle

Guide shingle

Bearing-guided bit follows profile of guide shingle.

Router-Scribed Shingles

I'VE SEEN A NUMBER OF TIPS for cutting outside corners on shingled walls, but none is as simple or foolproof as the method shown in the drawing at left. As illustrated, I use a bearing-guided flush-trimming bit in a small router to trim the overlapping shingle as the bearing follows the profile of the guide shingle.

—Will Hesch, Atascadero, Calif.

How to Hide Roofing Sealant

BLACK ROOFING SEALANT is a notoriously difficult goo to apply in a tidy manner to an asphalt-shingle roof. And if the sealant has to be used in a prominent place, it can be pretty unsightly. The next time this problem comes up, take a look in the gutters to see if there are deposits of gravel from the shingles. Collect a handful of gravel and dust it over the fresh sealant. It will blend the patch with the roof and protect the sealant from the elements.

—John Barton, New Market, Ala.

Solo Clapboard Hanging

WITH SIMPLE SITE-MADE HANGERS, I can handle unwieldy lengths of clapboard all by myself. As shown in the drawing at right, my little siding aids are made of two clear cedar shingles, butts pointing toward one another, with a 1-in. offset. The offset allows me to check the fit of the abutting clapboards. I make several hangers for a job, and I scribe alignment marks on them to correspond with the overlap of the clapboards.

I place the hangers vertically on the wall, aligning the marks with the bottom edges of the last course of clapboards. I attach the hangers with two short deck screws run through finishing washers. Using two screws will keep a hanger from pivoting and jamming as I position a clapboard on the house.

I install a clapboard from below, lifting it until the bottom of the clapboard reaches the lip formed by the butt of the bottom shingle. At that point, the springiness of the shingle pops the hanger under the clapboard, holding it in place. Now I'm free to slide the clapboard as needed to determine cut marks. To remove a clapboard, I just give it an outward twist at the top edge. This springs the shingle away from the wall, allowing me to drop the clapboard out of the hanger from any distance on the wall.

—Chris Ellis, Brewster, Mass.

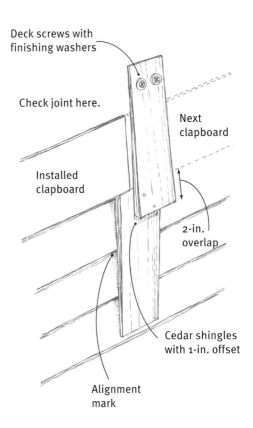

Deck screws with finishing washers

Check joint here.

Next clapboard

Installed clapboard

2-in. overlap

Cedar shingles with 1-in. offset

Alignment mark

Carpet on the Roof

I USE A COUPLE OF PIECES OF INDOOR-OUTDOOR CARPET to protect the shingles whenever I have some work to do on a roof. For example, I recently reshingled the sides of a dormer, and I used a 6-ft. by 8-ft. piece of the carpet as a place to kneel as I worked and to spread my tools on. The rubberized backing on the carpet grips the shingles like a pair of hiking boots, and the stuff is soft enough to be a lot more comfortable than pressing my knees against the abrasive hide of an asphalt shingle. Also, a light-colored carpet makes a much cooler place to work than a field of dark shingles soaking up the sun.

—Bart Balog, Cranston, R.I.

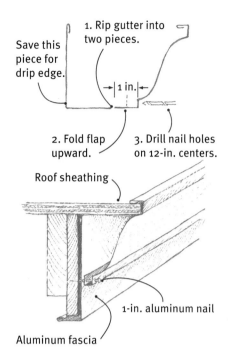

1. Rip gutter into two pieces.

Save this piece for drip edge.

← 1 in. →

2. Fold flap upward.

3. Drill nail holes on 12-in. centers.

Roof sheathing

1-in. aluminum nail

Aluminum fascia

Zero-Maintenance Crown Molding

I RECENTLY ENCLOSED THE PORCH ON OUR HOUSE, and in doing so I needed a crown molding for the gable-end bargeboards. I didn't have to look far. By ripping some lengths of aluminum gutter, as shown in the drawing at left, I was able to fashion inexpensive, zero-maintenance crown moldings that match the gutters.

I ripped the gutter into two portions, leaving a 1-in.-wide flap on the crown-molding pieces. I bent this flap by hand over a piece of ½-in. stock. Then I drilled through this folded edge on 12-in. centers for nails. The rest of the gutter? I'll use it for drip edges on my next project.

—Jack Murphy, Pittsburgh, Pa.

Tar Paper in High Winds

SOMETIMES YOU'VE GOT TO GET A HOUSE DRIED in before the roofers can install the shingles. Here in Wyoming, where the wind has been known to blow, builders usually tack hundreds of strips of wood lath over a roof covered with tar paper to keep the wind from picking the tar paper off. But then you've got to take the lath off again before the shingles can go on. Here's a better way.

On our last job we used tie wire, dispensed from a reel and held down by air-driven staples. First we stapled down the tar paper, using a hammer tacker. Then we ran the wire over all butt seams and lap seams between the sheets of tar paper and fastened the wire to the decking with staples on 12-in. centers. This system is a lot faster than putting down wood lath, and it holds the paper down extremely well. Best of all, when the roofers show up, they can put the shingles down right over the wire.

—Mark Kerridge, Casper, Wyo.

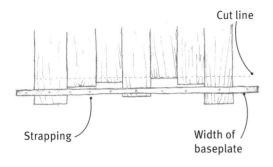

Cut line

Strapping

Width of baseplate

Trimming Siding

WHENEVER I FINISH A BUILDING'S exterior with vertical tongue-and-groove, shiplap, or rough-board siding, I use the method shown below to make straight, neat cuts. Every 3 ft. or 4 ft., I leave a board long by 4 in. to 6 in. Then I snap a chalkline about 1¾ in. down from my intended line of cut. This dimension is the width of my saw's baseplate from its edge to the blade. A piece of strapping tacked below this chalkline gives me a ready-made saw guide that will produce a crisp, straight line on the board ends.

—Bruce MacDougall, Bridgewater, N.H.

Controlling Roof Moss

NEXT TIME YOU SEE A WOOD OR ASPHALT ROOF that is furry with moss, mold, fungus, or algae, look around the chimney flashings. You'll probably see that there's nothing growing on the shingles in areas where rainwater washes across the copper or zinc flashings, and then onto the shingles. The same protection can be had on the entire roof by slipping pieces of zinc or copper flashing under the top row of shingles. Leave about half of the flashing's width exposed to the weather. That way rainwater can run across the metal and kill that nasty roof vegetation.

—Jefferson Kolle, Ridgefield, Conn.

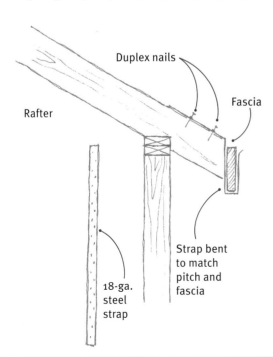

Duplex nails

Fascia

Rafter

18-ga. steel strap

Strap bent to match pitch and fascia

Help for Solo Fascia Hangers

TO HOLD THE OTHER END OF A LONG FASCIA BOARD, try a steel strap. As shown in the drawing at left, I bent an 18-ga. strap to conform to the profile of my fascia and the slope of the roof. Tacked on with a couple of duplex nails, the strap holds the unwieldy end of the fascia while I work toward it with my hammer.

—Glenn L. Miller, Wrightwood, Calif.

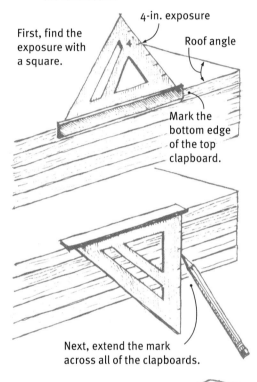

Rake board

Problem: Lay out and gang-cut the clapboards between the window and the rake board.

First, find the exposure with a square.

4-in. exposure

Roof angle

Mark the bottom edge of the top clapboard.

Next, extend the mark across all of the clapboards.

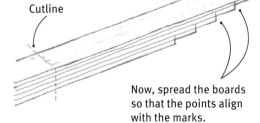

Cutline

Now, spread the boards so that the points align with the marks.

Gang-Cutting Angled Clapboards

THE NEXT TIME YOU'RE CUTTING CLAPBOARDS that run from a vertical window or sidewall to a rake board, try this trick. Cut the roof angle on one end of five clapboards (I stack them and cut them all at once with an 8-in. circular saw).

While the points of the clapboards are still lined up, slide a square along the bottom edge of the top clapboard. As shown in the second drawing from the top at left, align the exposure mark (in this case 4 in.) with the edge of the clapboard end. Now mark the edge of the clapboard, flip the square, and extend the mark across all of the clapboards, as shown in the third drawing from the top at left. Slide the boards so that the pointed ends line up with the marks above them, as shown in the bottom drawing at left. Measure the first clapboard, and you're ready to make the cut (I suggest a 10-in. power miter saw for this). After about 15 clapboards, it's a good idea to remeasure because errors have a tendency to accumulate.

—Randall Smith, Barrington, N.H.

9

Insulation

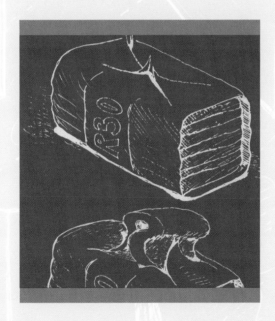

Wall-Sheathing Insulation Stops

I SWITCHED TO BLOWN-IN CELLULOSE INSULATION in attics of new homes a few years ago. Watching the installers prepping one job, I saw the trouble they had to go to stapling cardboard insulation stops between the rafters or trusses above the exterior-wall plates to keep the insulation from falling down into the soffit.

I came up with the idea, shown in the drawing at right, of letting the exterior-wall sheathing extend above the top plate and become an integral insulation stop when I was framing my next house. Instead of trimming 1 ft. off the last row of the sheathing to end it flush with the top plates, I decided to let it run above the plate. I calculated the height between the bottom and top truss chords at the point above the outside face of the exterior wall. Then I deducted 1½ in. from the distance to leave a ventilation slot between the top of the wall sheathing and the underside of the roof sheathing, and cut off the rest.

After the wall sheathing was nailed on, I marked the roof-truss layout along the top edge of the sheathing and squared down the lines to the top-plate level. Then, before lifting the walls, I cut 1¾-in. slots for each truss to drop into.

The slots had an added benefit for truss installation: They quickly positioned each truss and allowed me to float the walls beneath until they could be tweaked straight. Then I could nail down the trusses.

I used expanding spray foam to seal any gaps between the truss and the wall sheathing so that no insulation would slip by. All in all, the extra work saved me more than it cost me in time because the insulators didn't have to charge for crawling on their bellies to staple up cardboard stops. And I think it's a better detail.

—Mike Guertin, East Greenwich, R.I.

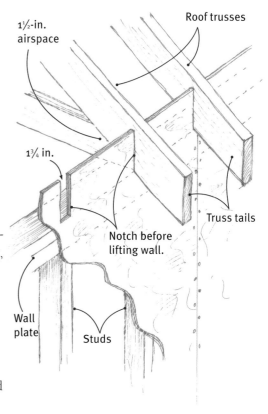

1½-in. airspace

Roof trusses

1¾ in.

Truss tails

Notch before lifting wall.

Wall plate

Studs

Cutting Insulation

MY PARTNER AND I PREFER USING A MACHETE to cut insulation. We bought ours for about $8 at the local hardware store. The cutting is done with the rounded part of the blade near the tip, with long, light pull strokes. Because it cuts cleanly, drifting bits of fiberglass dust are kept to a minimum. The tool has to be sharp, but it's easy to put a keen edge on the blade with a flat mill-bastard file.

—George Mines and Brent Spohn, Ganges, British Columbia

Storing Fiberglass Blankets

AS A REMODELING CARPENTER, I always have trouble using up a whole bundle of insulation. And once the bundle is opened, the blankets puff up to many times their compressed size. So if I don't use all of them, I end up with a pile of insulation that presents a storage problem.

The solution was inspired by a box of facial tissues. As shown in the drawing at right, I made an X-shaped slit across the top of a bundle of insulation just large enough to extract the top blanket. Then the rest of the blankets came out one at a time, just like tissues, while the remaining blankets stayed compact. By the way, this trick will only work with fiberglass blankets that come packaged in 4-ft. or 8-ft. lengths.

—Scott Knowles, Visalia, Calif.

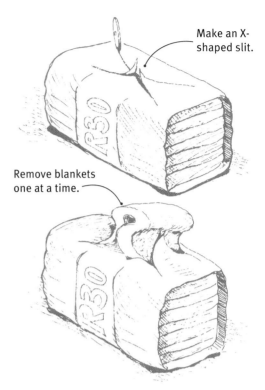

Make an X-shaped slit.

Remove blankets one at a time.

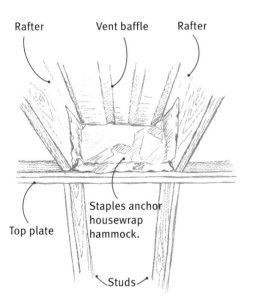

Rafter

Vent baffle

Rafter

Staples anchor housewrap hammock.

Top plate

Studs

Housewrap Hammocks for Insulation

HERE'S A MONEY-SAVING IDEA for insulating a cathedral ceiling. Although we're not required to put blocking between rafters along the plate line, we usually do so to keep the insulation from pushing down into the vented eave. On a recent job, we were short on 2x material. So I scrounged the housewrap scraps left over from our window cutouts and cut them into 10-in. by 30-in. strips for insulation supports.

As shown in the drawing at left, I folded the housewrap into a three-sided cradle and stapled the sides to the rafters and to the top plate. This setup created a sort of hammock to keep the insulation in place and took only a few seconds per rafter bay.

—Bob Swinburne, Brattleboro, Vt.

Cutting Insulation

I RECENTLY INSULATED MY ENTIRE HOUSE with foil-faced fiberglass batts, and I found a good tool for cutting the stuff down to size—hedge shears. That's right, but they have to be sharp. They easily cut through R-19 foil or kraft-paper faced batts even when they're fully lofted. You don't have to compress the insulation to cut it, as you would if you used a utility knife.

—Ron Smith, Sunol, Calif.

Carpet-Pad Insulation

ON A RECENT JOB replacing a pair of double-hung windows, I found myself looking for an insulative material to fill the gaps around the window frames. My search led me to some scraps of carpet padding that had been tossed into the Dumpster outside. Thinking I might have found the answer to the air-infiltration problem around the windows, I rescued some of the scraps and tried them out. Sure enough, the foam compressed well for a good fit without bowing the frame. Because the pad was made of recycled material, this use allowed it to be recycled again.

—Joe Archibald, Kitty Hawk, N.C.

10

Doors

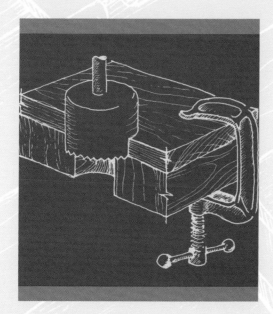

Door-Holding Jig

THIS IS A SKETCH OF A JIG I use to hold doors while routing them for hinges or planing them to fit. It automatically adjusts to doors of different thicknesses and holds them securely. The weight of the door provides the clamping action, and the return spring brings the clamp back into position.

—Kerry Ludden, Kearney, Neb.

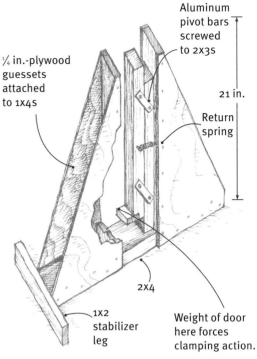

Aluminum pivot bars screwed to 2x3s

¼ in.-plywood guessets attached to 1x4s

21 in.

Return spring

2x4

1X2 stabilizer leg

Weight of door here forces clamping action.

Pivot Plates on Carpet

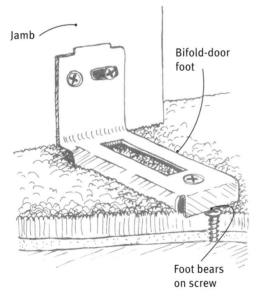

Jamb

Bifold-door foot

Foot bears on screw

IT CAN BE TOUGH TO INSTALL a bifold-door pivot foot over a carpeted floor—especially when the carpet is plush and the pad is thick. Even though the foot is affixed to the jamb, the horizontal leg doesn't have the solid bearing necessary to support the weight of a door. So people usually put a little block of wood under the foot, hoping that it will stay put and not be too noticeable.

The drawing at left shows the method I've developed to eliminate the little block of wood. First, I secure the foot plate to the jamb at the correct height with a screw driven partway into the oblong hole in the vertical leg. Then I swing the foot out of the way and drive another screw through the carpet and into the subfloor where the end of the foot will bear on the screw's head. I adjust this screw until its depth is right, then I run the screws into the side jamb on the vertical leg. The foot now has solid bearing, and the depth screw is practically invisible.

—Glenn J. Goldey, Colwyn, Pa.

Door-Trimming Jig

THE HINGE SIDE OF A DOOR must be trimmed to width at 90°. The latch side is usually trimmed at 5° off vertical for a beveled edge. Making these long cuts straight and smooth is easy with this two-sided jig.

First, buy a fine-toothed blade for your circular saw. I prefer a carbide-tipped plywood blade. Mount it on the saw arbor, and then use a combination square to make sure that the saw's base is 90° to the blade.

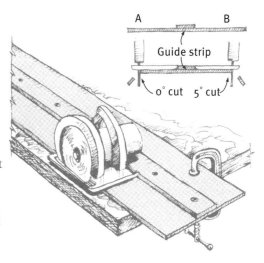

Build the jig with a ¼-in. Masonite, 8 ft. long and about 12 in. wide. Accurately place a straight Masonite guide strip, 2 in. wide, down the middle, gluing and tacking it firmly into position. Leave dimensions A and B large at first. When the glue is dry, trim the sides with your saw, one side with the blade set at 0°, the other side with the blade set at 5°. Mark the respective sides clearly. When the jig is clamped to the work, the appropriate edge will register the line of cut. For smooth operation, apply furniture wax or car wax to the surfaces on which the saw's baseplate slides.

For crossgrain cuts, first run a knife along the cutline to sever the surface fibers of the wood. This will eliminate splintering, which can be a problem with veneered doors.

—Philip Zimmerman, Berkeley, Calif.

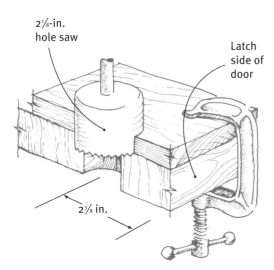

Lockset Retrofit

I RECENTLY HUNG SOME OLD DOORS that had been drilled to accept 1¾-in. locksets. These locksets needed replacing. To enlarge the old holes to house the new 2⅛-in. cylinder sets, I had to make a jig that would center my hole saw over the existing hole.

I took a scrap piece of ¾-in. stock, measured 2⅜ in. from the edge to allow for the standard setback, and drilled a hole with my 2⅛-in. hole saw. Then I clamped this guideboard over the existing hole, flush with the edge of the door, as shown at left. It acts as a guide for the outside of the hole saw itself, not for the arbor bit, and the holes come out clean and accurate.

—Mark Messier, Eugene, Ore.

Help for Hinges

A PERENNIAL PROBLEM WITH SOLID-CORE DOORS is that they are so heavy that they pull way from the jamb at the top hinge. To prevent this, I replace the two screws closest to the door stop with two 2½-in. or 3-in. wood screws, as shown in the drawing at right. (Drywall screws aren't a good choice, since they aren't plated to match and will eventually work loose because they aren't tapered.) It is important to get the screws as close as possible to the center of the jamb, or you run the risk of missing the trimmer stud. I hang new doors with the extra-long wood screws as a matter of course, and I find that it saves me a lot of planing on old doors that "don't fit any more."

—Sam Yoder, Cambridge, Mass.

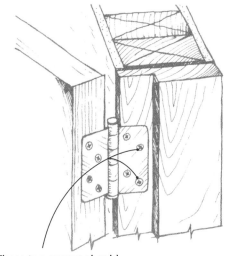

These two screws should extend into the stud.

Adjusting Doors

SOMETIMES A NEW DOOR WILL HANG COCKEYED in an old frame, despite the fact that the door and frame are properly sized, square, and plumb. This can happen if the depth of the hinge mortises is slightly off, if there's a twist in the jamb, or if there's any variation in the butts themselves.

To remedy this situation, most carpentry books advise shimming the hinges to throw the hinge pins closer to or farther from the jamb. This trial-and-error method takes quite a lot of time. Instead, simply close the door and remove the hinge pins from either the top and middle hinges, or bottom and middle hinges, and temporarily shim the bottom of the door so that the gap is even along both edges of the door. Now take a 6-in. adjustable wrench or smooth-jawed pliers, carefully bend the hinge knuckles until they once again align, and replace the pins. I know that this approach sounds brutal, but it does work. If necessary, you can pull a door as close as 1/32 in. of the jamb without making it hinge-bound. In fact, making minor adjustments with this method will automatically relieve the stiff action of bound hinges without ever having to loosen a screw or cut a cardboard shim.

—Dave Walter, Oakwood, Ill.

Screw-Clamp Door Buck

Sometimes we forget that a tool can be used to advantage for other than its original purpose—the ubiquitous screw clamp, for instance. I needed to plane the edge of a small door recently and found a pair of these clamps to be handy supports. By clamping one to each end of the door, as shown at right, I was able to brace the door while I planed its edge.

—L. Fredrick, Aspen, Colo.

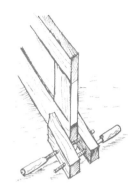

Easy Door Buck

BUILDING A DOOR BUCK IS A GOOD IDEA if you find yourself dealing with a house full of door hanging from scratch, but for a quick setup, the answer is right in your toolbox. I use two bar clamps, one on each side of the door. Small blocks between the clamp and the door face will prevent marring.

—Paul A. Jones, Pacifica, Calif.

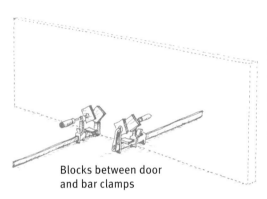

Blocks between door and bar clamps

Another Quick Buck

WHEN I HAVE TO BRACE A DOOR for hinge or lockset operations, I use a door buck made from scrap materials like the one in the drawing at right. The base is made of ½-in. plywood and a couple of 2x4 offcuts. It's important that the plywood be thin enough to bend a little under the weight of the door, which makes the 2x braces angle inward, pinching the door and holding it steady. If you're concerned about marring the finish of a door, make the gap between the braces a little wider and line the braces with strips of carpet.

—Ed Wilson, Seattle, Wash.

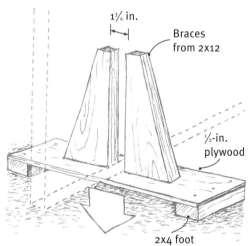

1¾ in.

Braces from 2x12

½-in. plywood

2x4 foot

Making a Quick Buck

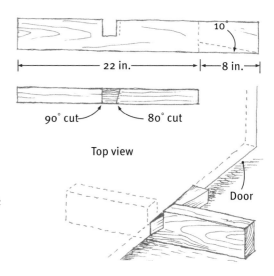

An Irish craftsman, with whom I had the pleasure of working, showed me how to make a simple door buck quickly. In fact, it's so easy to make that it could be considered disposable, but it's small enough that you might want to hang on to it.

Take a 30-in. 2x4 and make a 10° taper cut along the first 8 in. of the face, as shown in the drawing at right. Then make a crosscut at the 8-in. mark so that you have an 8-in. wedge with a 10° taper. Turn the 2x4 on edge and set your saw at a depth of 2 in. Make a 90° crosscut near the center of the board, then move over 2 in. and make another crosscut at 80°. Then make several passes with the saw between the two cuts, knock out the pieces, and clean up the slot with a chisel.

Slide a door into the slot in the 2x4 and drive in the wedge with a few taps. To keep the door from rocking, locate the buck toward one end of the door, or use one at each end.

—Tim Hoisington, Greenfield, Mass.

Chiseling Hinge Mortises

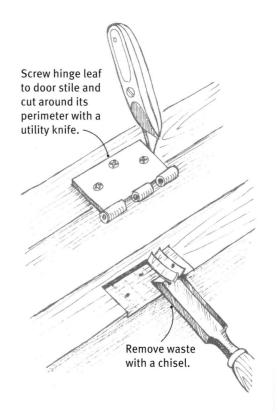

Screw hinge leaf to door stile and cut around its perimeter with a utility knife.

Remove waste with a chisel.

I TYPICALLY USE A ROUTER AND A TEMPLATE to cut mortises or to enlarge existing mortises for new door hinges. But for small jobs where it doesn't make sense to cart along a lot of gear, I use a utility knife and a chisel for the same purpose. First I screw the hinge to the door stile in the desired position. Then I score around the edges of the hinge with the knife as shown in the drawing at right. With the hinge removed, I chisel the mortise to the thickness of the hinge. Now I can reattach the hinge using the same screw holes.

—Daniel E. Hill, III, Griswold, Conn.

Hinge-Mortising Jig

I USE A ROUTER AND A JIG to mortise hinges in doors and casement windows. By using a ½-in.-dia. hinge-mortising bit and a standard round-cornered hinge, I achieve a consistently clean fit that would be difficult and slow to get by hand.

A piece of ⅜-in. plywood forms the base of the jig. After carefully measuring the size of the hinge and the router baseplate, I nail 1x1 fences to the base to guide the router. As the router is passed inside the bounds of the fences, the bit will cut the hinge shape into the plywood base. Once the mortise is cut out of the base, I lower the bit to adjust the depth of cut in the door.

A 1x2 edge guide nailed and glued to the base aligns the jig on the edge of the work. To keep the jig steady while using the router, I tack 6d nails through the plywood base into the edge of the door or window jamb.

—Steve Larson, Santa Cruz, Calif.

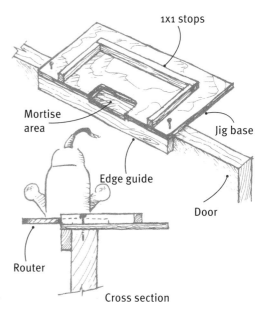

1x1 stops

Mortise area

Edge guide

Jig base

Door

Router

Cross section

Locating a Strike Plate

WHENEVER I INSTALL A LOCKSET, I rub a little bit of pencil lead on the edge of the latch, as shown in the drawing at right. Then I turn the knob to retract the latch, close the door until it's hard against the doorstop, and release the knob. The latch then bumps into the door jamb, leaving a graphite mark. This mark shows me where the leading edge of the strike plate should go.

—Sandy Tod, Lynden, Ontario

Rub pencil on latch edge.

Align edge of strike plate with pencil line.

Door

11

Drywall

Removing Drywall

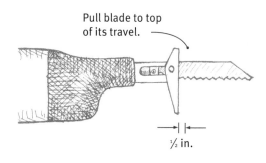

Pull blade to top of its travel.

½ in.

IF YOU'VE EVER HAD TO SLUG IT OUT with a wall to remove drywall for a remodeling project, you can appreciate how tedious it is. Faced with this problem on a recent job, I came up with the following method to cut the drywall into manageable chunks.

As shown in the drawing at left, I affixed an old, general-purpose wood-cutting blade to my reciprocating saw (after unplugging it, of course). Then I pulled the saw's drive shaft outward, to the limit of its travel, and marked a cutline on the blade ½ in. from the shoe. This represented the thickness of the drywall I was removing. Next I used a pair of cable pliers to cut the blade.

In use, I simply held the saw against the wall with its shoe flush against the surface. As I moved it up and down the wall, it punched a series of closely spaced holes in the drywall. Studs didn't interfere—the saw just passed right over them. In no time I had a tidy pile of ex-walls, without a cloud of asphyxiating dust.

—Patrick C. Perry, Lakewood, Colo.

Corner Patch

A FREQUENT PROBLEM IN REMODELING and repair work is the damaged outside corner where some plaster has chipped off, but not enough to warrant installing a corner bead. To fix these dings, I take a flat plasterer's trowel (ideally longer than the chipped area) and lay it on one side of the corner, flush to the edge, where it acts as a form. Then I fill the exposed side of the hole with patching compound and slide the trowel away from the corner without lifting it off the wall, as shown at right. For larger fill-ins, plaster works better because it doesn't sag as much as patching compound. When using plaster, be sure to apply water or a bonding agent to the old surface.

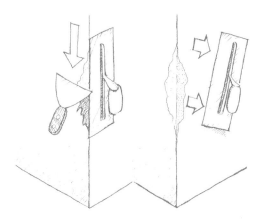

—Sam Yoder, Cambridge, Mass.

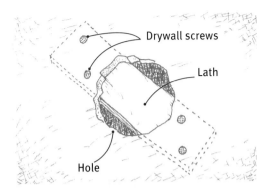

Drywall screws

Lath

Hole

Patching Drywall

HERE IS STILL ANOTHER WAY to install a drywall patch in a spot that doesn't have any backing. First, cut an oversize patch and nibble away at it until it fits the hole. Next, find a piece of plywood or lath that is longer but narrower than the hole. Slip the wood behind the drywall and position it so that it spans the hole, as shown in the drawing at left. Drive drywall screws through the wallboard and into the lath to draw it up tight to the back of the gypboard. Screw the patch to the lath, and you're ready to fill the cracks with joint compound.

—William Barstow, Arcata, Calif.

Cutting Drywall with a T-Square

I STUCK A HUNK OF ADHESIVE-BACKED 80-grit sandpaper on the back of my drywall square, as shown in the drawing at right. The sandpaper keeps the square's tongue from sliding around when I'm making my cut with a utility knife.

—Tim Brigham, Doylestown, Pa.

Sandpaper patch under T-square blade grips drywall during cuts.

Nail Pops

OFTEN AN ANNOYING NAIL POP on newly hung, taped, and painted drywall can be flattened without having to refill and paint it. I take a 6-in. taping knife and flatten it out over the pop. I then give a sharp rap with a hammer to the area of the knife over the pop, and at least half the time, the knife distributes the blow well enough to flatten the spot without marring the paint. A quarter of the time touch-up painting is required, and unfortunately, remaining instances will need recoating and repainting. But the odds are in favor of this technique, and I've never damaged a knife doing this.

—Robert H. Brereton, Minneapolis, Minn.

Invisible Drywall Buttjoints

During my 40 years in the trades, I've had a number of high-end dry-wall jobs that required dead-flat ceilings—no telltale bulges allowed where the ends of the drywall sheets abut one another. The method shown in the drawing at right is our solution to the problem. I've inspected some jobs that we did 25 years ago using this method, and you still can't see where the butt joints occur.

This drywall trick starts with a sheet of plywood. The plywood should be the same thickness as the drywall. First, trim an inch off the width of the sheet, then crosscut it into 10 equal strips. They will be 9¼ in. wide by 47 in. long. As shown in the drawing, we next staple strips of ⅟₁₆-in.-thick poster board to the long edges of the plywood strip.

Before raising a drywall panel for installation, we screw one of the plywood strips to the end of the panel. The poster-board strip goes be-tween the plywood and the drywall. As the drywall goes up, the butt ends are arranged to fall between the ceiling joists. When the adjacent drywall panel is screwed to the plywood strip, a shallow dip is created where the drywall bends over the poster board. This shallow dip creates a hollow for the tape.

We tape our joints in the usual manner, beginning with the butt joints. Once that joint compound has dried, we tape the long edges. Incidentally, a 20-in.-long piece of 1½-in. aluminum angle is a handy tool for lev-eling the finish coats of joint compound over the butt ends. Using this technique, we never had a joint show up on a punch list at the completion of a job.

—Tim Hanson, Indianapolis, Ind.

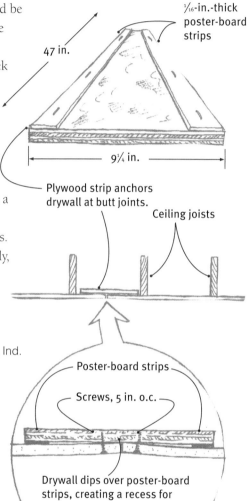

⅟₁₆-in.-thick poster-board strips

47 in.

9¼ in.

Plywood strip anchors drywall at butt joints.

Ceiling joists

Poster-board strips

Screws, 5 in. o.c.

Drywall dips over poster-board strips, creating a recess for tape and joint compound.

Avoiding Cracks in Drywalled Cathedral Ceilings

CRACKS OFTEN DEVELOP at the peak of a cathedral ceiling because the wood framing members move around a little with seasonal changes. The intersecting planes of drywall move along with the framing (be they rafters or scissor trusses), and the taped joint at the peak just isn't sturdy enough to stay intact for long. The drawing at right shows a method I use to cope with such a problem.

Prior to installing the drywall, I fasten a strip of sturdy metal flashing to one side of the ceiling. The flashing is bent to conform to the shape of the roof and extends 8 in. to 10 in. down both sides from the peak. Next, I secure the drywall to the ceiling to which the flashing is anchored. This side goes up in the normal manner, with the drywall screwed to the rafters all the way to the peak. The detail changes, however, on the other side. Within a foot of the peak, I screw the drywall to the sheet metal but not to the roof framing. This method relocates stress points to the fasteners in the field of the drywall rather than the taped joint along its edges.

—Gary Wray, Coupeville, Wash.

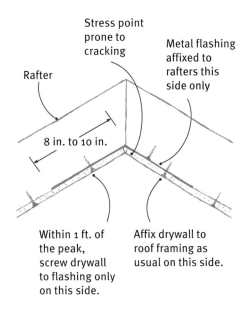

Stress point prone to cracking

Metal flashing affixed to rafters this side only

Rafter

8 in. to 10 in.

Within 1 ft. of the peak, screw drywall to flashing only on this side.

Affix drywall to roof framing as usual on this side.

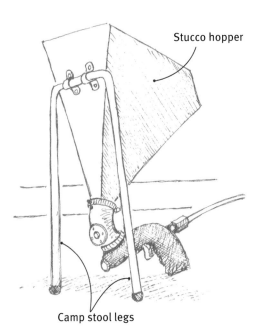

Stucco hopper

Camp stool legs

Hopper Prop

I'VE BEEN CUSSING MY SPRAY-STUCCO HOPPER for years because it has to be propped up or set in a bucket every time I put it down for a refill or change its position. Then I saw a folding camp stool in my pile of aluminum recycling scraps. I cut the rivets that held the two halves of the stool together and attached one pair of legs to the hopper with pipe hangers and a couple of pop rivets, as shown in the drawing at left. The tight-fitting hangers hold the legs in any position, and now my hopper sits wherever I put it, like a good dog.

—Dave Echeverria, Corral De Tierra, Calif.

A Self-Mudding Drywall-Tape Dispenser

I'VE HAD PEOPLE GIVE ME some pretty strange looks when I carry my drywall-taping machine onto a job site. But the machine's looks are deceiving. As shown in the drawing at right, I built the unit out of scrap 2x4s, a 2x6, and a 1-gal. plastic bucket. The bucket is affixed to the 2x6 crossbar with four short screws.

I made two slits in the side of the bucket where they engage the bottom. The slits are on opposite sides. The rear slit should be large enough just to allow the tape to pass through it. The front slit should be slightly wider to allow both the tape and a thin layer of joint compound to pass through it.

A roll of paper tape hangs from the 2x4 upright toward the back of the rig. I run the tape through the slits in the bucket, and then I fill the bucket with thinned joint compound. Now I'm ready to pull the tape out to my desired length, lop it off with a razor knife, and apply it directly to the wall—no premudding necessary. Using this setup, two of us taped a 1,100-sq.-ft. house in five hours.

—Chris Matishak,
Delburne, Alberta

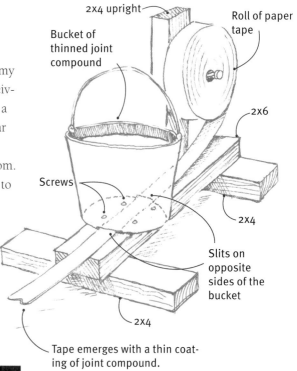

Labels: 2x4 upright · Roll of paper tape · Bucket of thinned joint compound · 2x6 · Screws · 2x4 · Slits on opposite sides of the bucket · 2x4 · Tape emerges with a thin coating of joint compound.

Little Batches of Drywall Compound

NEXT TIME YOU NEED just a little amount of setting-type drywall compound, try this. Place the amount of dry compound you think you will need in a 1-gal. heavy-duty Ziploc bag. Now add half the amount of water you think is necessary and knead the mixture. Add small amounts of water until you get the desired consistency. When you're done, turn the bag inside out, brush off the flakes, and save it for another batch.

—Charles Jefferson, Salem, Ore.

Standout Drywall Touch-Ups

NO MATTER HOW GOOD YOUR DRYWALL-TAPING SKILLS ARE, chances are you'll find a missed dimple or two in the final sanding. I used to circle the dimples with a pencil, touch them up with joint compound, and sand them once they'd had a chance to dry—just like everyone else.

For some reason, though, I found that I often forgot to sand these touch-ups. They blended in so well that I didn't discover them until I had a paint-brush in hand, and one time it took a critical client to bring one of those forgotten touch-ups to my attention.

I've solved this problem with a little bit of paint. I mix some into my touch-up mud so that when the stuff dries, the patch stands out. This result always seems to raise a question from the curious client, instead of the critical one.

—Rick Newman, Tupper Lake, N.Y.

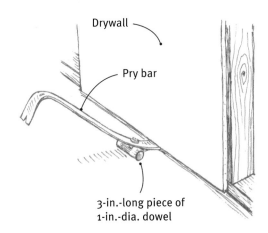

Drywall

Pry bar

3-in.-long piece of
1-in.-dia. dowel

Drywall Kicker

IN THE COURSE OF MY CONSTRUCTION PROJECTS I have to hang some drywall once in a while, but not often enough to justify investing in a real drywall "kicker"—a lever device made especially for lifting a piece of drywall. Instead, I modified my pry bar as shown in the drawing at left to do the same task. Through its nail-pulling hole I attached a 3-in. length of 1-in.-dia. dowel with a bolt that is countersunk in the dowel. Voilà! With just a little toe pressure, I can lift a drywall panel 2 in. off the floor with this tool.

—Andrew Kirk, Independence, Calif.

12

Trim & Finish Carpentry

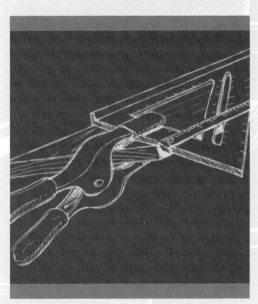

Forming Curved Trim

TRIMMING ARCHED WINDOWS CAN BE A PROBLEM, especially with complex molding patterns. This method requires two pieces of molding to form one finished piece of curved, paint-grade trim.

First, determine the distance between the inside edges of the vertical moldings (let's say 4 ft.). Cut the appropriate radius out of a sheet of plywood thicker than the trim and nail it to a plywood base. Our 4-ft.-dia. arch will need a 2¾-in. trim piece a little over 7 ft. long, cut from two 8 ft. pieces (A and B in the drawing at right) to allow a margin of error.

Remove material the width of the sawblade (the kerf) from the edge of piece B and then set the table-saw fence to leave a strip exactly one kerf wide with each pass. You don't have to remove the fence again. Running the two pieces through the saw alternately makes it easier to collate the thin strips. If your molding has a hollow back, tack shims in the jig, one foot on center, to ensure proper alignment during clamping. Baste the strips with your favorite glue, place them in sequence against the curved form, and clamp the steel strap in place. I use a 26-ga. steel strap cut from an old downspout for a clamp; one end is nailed to the base, and the other has a loop large enough to anchor the end of a bar clamp. A bar clamp is better than a C-clamp for this application because the sliding jaw allows tensioning without exhausting the reach of the threaded shaft.

When the glue has set, scrape off the excess and sandpaper the rough edges. The junction with the vertical trim should be a 90° cut in the base of the arch at the point tangent to vertical.

—Jud Peake, Oakland, Calif.

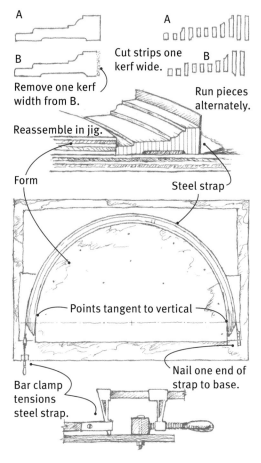

A
B
Remove one kerf width from B.
Cut strips one kerf wide.
A
B
Run pieces alternately.
Reassemble in jig.
Form
Steel strap
Points tangent to vertical
Nail one end of strap to base.
Bar clamp tensions steel strap.

Spring-Loaded Dowels

I CAME UP WITH THIS SIMPLE WAY to dowel a rail in place between two fixed posts. Drill and dowel one end of the rail as you normally would. On the other end, drill the hole deeper and insert a spring before the dowel. Make the depth of the hole equal to the length of the dowel plus the length of the compressed spring.

Once it's aligned with the hole in the post, the spring-loaded dowel will push its way home. I butter the dowel with hide glue before inserting it in the rail. I also drill a small vent hole in the bottom of the rail to prevent suction problems. Beveling the ends of the dowel allows the parts to go together easily.

—Thomas Ehlers, Austin, Tex.

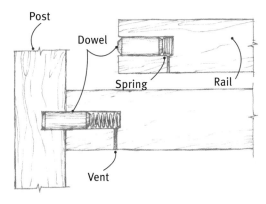

Post
Dowel
Spring
Rail
Vent

Cutting Double-Angle Miters

RECENTLY THE GENERAL CONTRACTOR I work for was low bidder on the finish phase of a large Victorian-style office building. The job called for crown moldings, 20 raised-panel doors surrounded by 4-in. casings, and hundreds of feet of 7-in.-high baseboard. Both the baseboard and the casing had a ⅜-in. Roman ogee milled on one edge. At each doorway, the base and casing were to be mitered. The miter where the ogees met at the top of the joint was 45°, but this angle changed on the flat face of the trim pieces as shown at right. The question was how to cut a lot of these double-angle miters with speed and accuracy.

I solved the problem by drawing the joints full size (both right-hand and left-hand sides) on ⅜-in. plywood, and then cutting each one apart along the lines of the intersection. I added stops along the ogee-edge side of each pattern, making it easy to align them with the stock. Clamping the stock and patterns together as shown in the drawing, I cut each joint with a small router using a ¼-in. bearing-overcutter bit. Armed with these guide jigs, the rest of the crew joined me in production-cutting the miters.

—Bob Grace, San Jose, Calif.

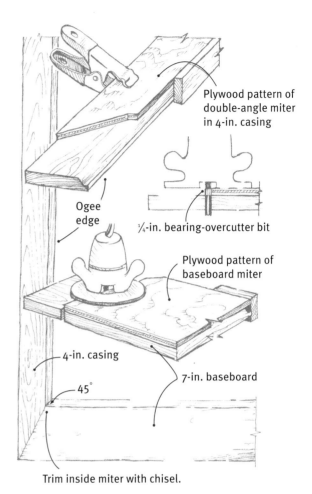

Plywood pattern of double-angle miter in 4-in. casing

Ogee edge

¼-in. bearing-overcutter bit

Plywood pattern of baseboard miter

4-in. casing

7-in. baseboard

45°

Trim inside miter with chisel.

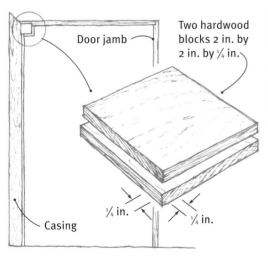

Door jamb

Two hardwood blocks 2 in. by 2 in. by ¼ in.

Casing

¼ in.

¼ in.

Casing Reveal Gauge

WHENEVER I INSTALL DOOR OR WINDOW CASINGS, I use the jig shown at left to make sure that I get an accurate ¼-in. reveal. It's made of two square pieces of hardwood, ¼ in. thick, that are glued together with a ¼-in. offset. This jig has so many corners that half the time I grab it out of my nail bag, it's in the right position for use.

—John Sandstrom, Fort Dodge, Iowa

Baseboard Splice

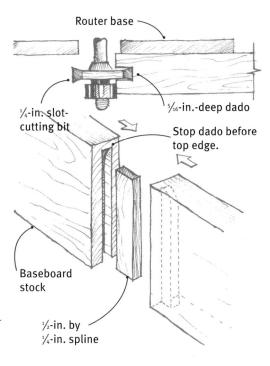

Router base

¼-in. slot-cutting bit

⁵⁄₁₆-in.-deep dado

Stop dado before top edge.

Baseboard stock

½-in. by ¼-in. spline

WHEN I NEED LONG RUNS OF 1X BASEBOARD, I don't splice my boards with 45° scarf joints. Instead, I cut the boards square, letting the breaks fall where they may regardless of stud layout, and I join the pieces with small splines.

I use a ¼-in. slot-cutting bit in my router to cut a ⁵⁄₁₆-in.-deep dado in the end of each board. Care has to be taken here to avoid cutting through the top edge of the baseboard stock. Then I spread glue on a ½-in. by ¼-in. spline that is slightly shorter than the length of the dado, insert it in one of the dadoes, and tap another board onto it. The result is a perfect, tight-fitting, no-fuss joint.

With this method, you save time by not having to cut, adjust, and recut the mitered joint, and you save material by not having to break the baseboards over a stud. You also avoid the inevitable splitting when you nail mitered joints together without predrilling them.

—Robert Prasch, Portland, Ore.

Baseboards for Tile Floors

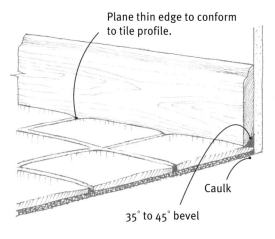

Plane thin edge to conform to tile profile.

Caulk

35° to 45° bevel

THE COST OF TILE COVE BASE is surprisingly high—about $3 to $4 per running foot. On the other hand, scribing a wooden baseboard to a tile floor is very time-consuming. The method I use to install wooden baseboards gives me a water-resistant joint where tile and wood meet, and a fit that looks painstakingly scribed, but isn't.

First, I bevel the back of my baseboard material as shown in the drawing at left. The thin edge on the front of the baseboard will usually conform to a well-laid tile floor with a few taps of a hammer—no scribing is necessary. Be sure to use a piece of scrap wood to cushion the hammer blows.

After dry-fitting, I tack the baseboards in place. As I remove them one at a time, I carefully lay a bead of good caulking compound in the void behind the bevel. I like Geocel caulk (Box 398, Elkhart, Ind. 46515). Any caulk that oozes out can be cut away after it sets up. Prefinishing the baseboards saves time and usually gives better results than trying to paint or varnish them in place.

—M. Felix Marti, Monroe, Ore.

Hanger-Bolt Driver

TO SCREW IN RAIL BOLTS EASILY, make up a driver from a threaded rod connector and two setscrews. You can determine the length of the installed stud by how far you drive the setscrews into the rod connector. Screw the rail bolt into one end of the connector. Then use a socket and ratchet or electric drill on the other end to drive the bolt into its pilot hole. A touch of paraffin on the screw threads will make the job easier.

—Alan Dorr, Chico, Calif.

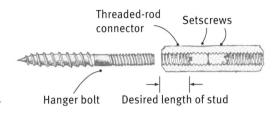

Threaded-rod connector   Setscrews

Hanger bolt   Desired length of stud

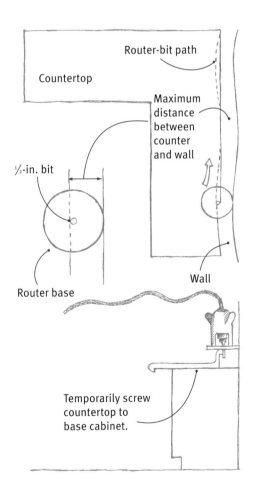

Countertop

Router-bit path

Maximum distance between counter and wall

½-in. bit

Router base

Wall

Temporarily screw countertop to base cabinet.

Router-Scribing Countertops

AS A KITCHEN-CABINET INSTALLER, I have scribed hundreds of countertops to fit irregular walls. Most require very little removal of material, but some require that I carve away as much as ½ in. of material, which is a long, dirty job with a belt sander.

Now I use a new technique that leaves the old way in the dust. As shown in the drawing at left, I use a medium-duty router with a ½-in.-dia. straight-shank cutter. The countertop is held back from the wall and is temporarily screwed from below to the base cabinets. At the maximum distance between the counter and the wall, the bit should just kiss the very edge of the counter.

Next, I run the router across the backsplash scribe using the wall as a guide. Apart from a minor touch-up in the corner with a belt sander, the job is complete. A perfect fit, every time.

—Steven Morris, Sarnia, Ontario

Moldings on Masonry Walls

THE DRAWING AT RIGHT ILLUSTRATES THE METHOD that I use to apply trim pieces, such as chair railings, to a concrete, brick, or block wall. I do it this way because it allows me to use finish nails to secure the work to the wall. Then the nail holes can easily be filled to match a natural or stained finish.

First I drive nails into the railing so that their tips just begin to emerge on the backside. Then I hold the railing in place on the wall and drive the nails far enough to make marks. Next I drill ¾-in. holes in the masonry, using the nail marks as centerpoints. I fill each hole with a piece of ¾-in. dowel that has been kerfed on one end with a bandsaw. If I'm working on a concrete block wall with open cells, I make sure that the dowel is long enough to bear against the far inside wall of the block.

Once the dowels are wedged in place and trimmed flush with the wall, I affix the railing to the wall by driving the nails into the dowels.

—Jim Stuart, Covina, Calif.

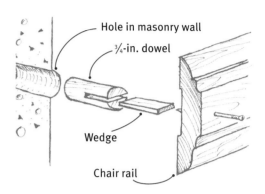

Hole in masonry wall

¾-in. dowel

Wedge

Chair rail

- -

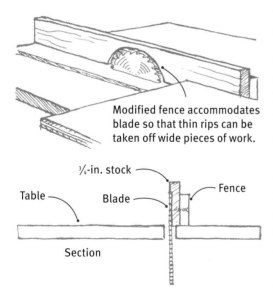

Modified fence accommodates blade so that thin rips can be taken off wide pieces of work.

¾-in. stock

Table

Blade

Fence

Section

Close Shaves on the Table Saw

WHENEVER I DO FINISH CARPENTRY ON SITE, I use a small, portable table saw for everything from trim to cabinet work. Unfortunately, the diminutive table limits the width of the work that can be passed by the blade. Sometimes I have to take minuscule rips off the edge of a large piece of plywood, so I devised the modified fence shown in the drawing at left to allow close shaves on the little saw.

To modify the fence, I screwed a ¾-in.-thick, knot-free piece of wood to the blade side of the fence, making sure that the screws were well away from the path of the sawblade. Then with the blade lowered below the level of the table, I positioned the wood so that it was flush with the outside edge of the blade. I turned the saw on and slowly raised the blade to full height, cutting a half-moon void in the wood fence.

I use this fence along with an 80-tooth carbide blade to take 64ths off wide stock.

—Jeffrey S. Janssen, Oakland, Calif.

Locating Latches

HERE'S A FAST, ACCURATE METHOD that I use for locating the center-points for door latch and dead-bolt mortises. First I center a hole for a 6d nail in the end of a short piece of dowel (a 1-in.-dia. dowel for a typical lockset). Then I drive the nail partway into the hole, cut it off, and sharpen the remaining shank to a point.

After boring the holes for the lockset in the door's stile, I insert the dowel into the hole that will contain the latch tube, as shown in the drawing at right. Then I close the door and simply push the dowel marker toward the jamb. The sharpened nail marks the exact centerpoint for my latch or bolt hole.

—Bernard H. King, Mechanicville, N.Y.

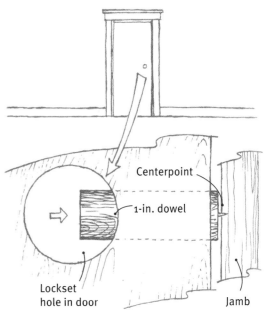

Centerpoint

1-in. dowel

Lockset hole in door

Jamb

Joining Stair Rails

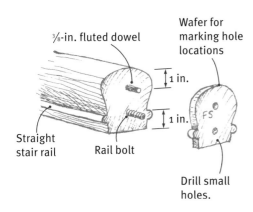

⅜-in. fluted dowel

Wafer for marking hole locations

1 in.

1 in.

FS

Straight stair rail

Rail bolt

Drill small holes.

IN THE PAST I JOINED SECTIONS OF STRAIGHT STAIR RAIL to fittings in the typical fashion.

I used the rail bolt that came with the fitting, with a hex nut instead of the furnished star nut. But frequently during installation of the assembled rail sections, the glue line would break from the shock of coaxing the rail onto the balusters with a rubber mallet, or from the twisting action of aligning the rail with the newel posts. Then I'd have to reglue and contour the joint all over again. I remedied this situation by adding a ⅜-in. dowel to the joint, as shown in the drawing at left. I use a wafer, cut from a section of rail, to mark the location of both the hole for the rail bolt and the dowel hole. To make sure I don't compound any error in the placement of the holes, I mark an "FS" on one side of the wafer to indicate the "fitting side," and I take care to orient it correctly. In addition to strengthening the joint to withstand the strain of installation, the dowel resists the torquing action of tightening the nut during assembly, helping to maintain proper alignment of the parts. Since I started using this method, I haven't had to rework a single joint.

—D. B. Lovingood, Suffolk, Va.

Arch Trammel

HERE IS A TECHNIQUE that I have found handy for laying out wide, shallow arches. I discovered it at a shipyard, where boatbuilders use it for laying out the rounded camber of boat decks.

On a clear, flat wood surface, such as a subfloor, draw a straight line as long as the arch will be wide, as shown in the drawing at right. Drive a finish nail at each end of this baseline, so that about 1 in. of the nail's shank projects above the floor. Find the center of the baseline and draw a perpendicular line extending up from the center, making an inverted T. Decide the height of your arch, measure along the perpendicular line from the baseline, and drive a third finish nail at the apex.

Now find two straight 1x boards, each one a little longer than the length of the baseline. Snug one board against one base nail and the apex nail, and lay the other board against the other base nail and the apex nail. Where the boards overlap, mark them for a half-lap joint. Then cut the joint and screw the boards together.

Pull out the apex nail and hold a pencil in its place. Now slide the boards along the baseline nail guides from right to left to mark the arch. As a variation, you can mount a router at the apex and cut or mold arches of any size.

—Jerry Azevedo, Corvallis, Ore.

Half-lap joint secured with screws

Nail guide at apex

Nail guide

Nail guide

Baseline

Resulting arch

Pencil

Remove nail at apex and slide trammel along, pivoting on nail guides, to describe arc.

Plastic Laminate on Two Sides

TO APPLY PLASTIC LAMINATE on both faces of a cabinet door, you can save yourself some time by doing them simultaneously. Drill a hole at each corner of the door, 1 in. to 2 in. from the edges, and drive a small wood screw a few turns into each hole. Apply contact cement to the side with screws, then turn it over so that the door is supported on the screw feet. Apply cement to the other side of the door, and to the laminated pieces. When the cement is tacky, apply the laminate to the side without the screws. Flip the door, take out the screws, laminate the second side, and you're ready to finish the edges with a trim bit in a router.

—Roy T. Higa, Honolulu, Hawaii

Riser and Tread Marking Gauge

It would be nice if the treads and risers in a site-built stair could all be the same, but the vagaries of wood-frame construction usually mean that uniform lengths and 90° angles are as often exceptions as they are rules. To get accurate measurements for treads and risers that vary by just a little bit, I use the marking gauge shown in the drawing at right. It consists of two end pieces and a crossbar, all made of ½-in. particleboard. The end pieces are secured to the crossbar with nuts, washers, and four ¼-in. flat-head machine screws, which protrude through oblong slots in the crossbar. The slots allow the end pieces to be moved in and out until they make a snug fit with the skirt boards—even if they are a bit out of square. Once the fit is right, I tighten the nuts and transfer the entire gauge to the riser or tread stock, where I can mark the exact layout without making any tedious measurements.

—James M. Westerholm, Seattle, Wash.

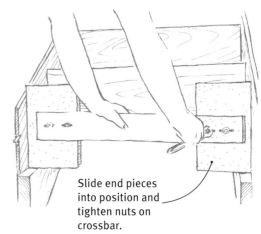

Slide end pieces into position and tighten nuts on crossbar.

Acute Angles on the Chop Saw

A couple of years ago I was doing some trim with my friend Marcos Bradley. He was running base around a series of odd angles—angles he couldn't readily cut with his chop saw. After some thought he assembled a jig similar to the one shown in the drawing at left. Use clamps or screws to secure one of the jig's fences to the saw's fence. Clamp the workpiece to the jig (block under the far end of long pieces), and you're all set to cut accurate acute angles.

—M. Felix Marti, Monroe, Ore.

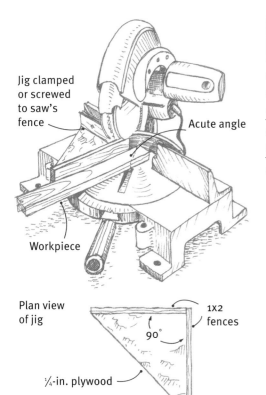

Jig clamped or screwed to saw's fence

Acute angle

Workpiece

Plan view of jig

1X2 fences

90°

¼-in. plywood

Raising Panels with a Router

I USE THE VERTICAL RAISED PANEL BIT because I was intimidated by the great whirling mass of steel that is the horizontal bit. But I was also dissatisfied with the wavy cut that often results when using the vertical bit. It's just difficult to hold the panel absolutely flat to a vertical fence.

To regain the advantage of a horizontal work surface, I mounted my router at 90° to the conventional setup. As shown in the drawing, I affixed the router to a piece of hardwood plywood. The base of the router rests in a shallow recess routed into the plywood. The plywood mounting plate is attached to a 2-in.-thick top by way of two ¼-in.-dia. machine screws driven into threaded inserts embedded in the top. One screw acts as a pivot point. The other projects through a slot in the mounting plate. A washer and a large knob on this screw allow the mounting plate to be clamped at the desired height relative to the work surface. The router bit should be below the work as the panel is passed over it, and the cut should start out shallow and be increased gradually until the final depth is reached. Notice that the locking point is twice as far from the pivot point as the center of the router bit. At this relationship, raising the plate ¼ in. at the locking point lifts the bit ⅛ in. I made some marks on the back of the mounting plate to act as a depth scale, which makes it quick and easy to gauge the depth of the cut.

—Donald C. Brown, Ruckersville, Va.

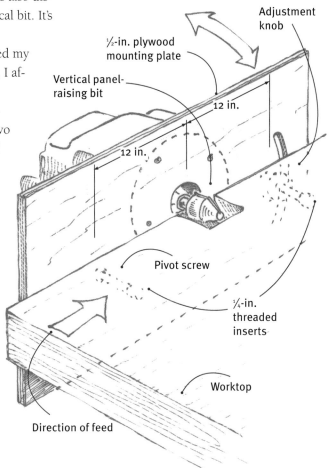

Adjustment knob

½-in. plywood mounting plate

Vertical panel-raising bit

12 in.

12 in.

Pivot screw

¼-in. threaded inserts

Worktop

Direction of feed

Getting a Grip on Miters

I DO PLENTY OF TRIM WORK, and I often have to measure from the short point of a miter. I've come up with an easy way to get accurate measurements every time. As shown in the drawing at left, I place my Speed Square across the short end of the miter. Then I secure the square to the workpiece with a squeeze of my spring clamp, hook my tape measure on the square, and pull my measurement.

—Greg Smith, Snowmass, Colo.

Speed Square flush with short end of miter

Plugging a Toe-Screw

DURING THE COURSE OF MY WORK, which is primarily finish carpentry, I find it necessary to angle a screw in toenail fashion from time to time. A typical example is the intersection of a handrail with a wall. The problem is that if the screw is countersunk and counterbored, the angled counterbore can't be easily capped with a plug or a button.

I solve this problem by first drilling a larger counterbore—usually ½-in.—at a right angle to the surface of the stock. I make this hole as shallow as possible. As shown in the drawing at right, the second counterbore—usually ⅜- in.—begins inside the larger counterbore and angles toward the anchoring surface.

It takes a little practice to know exactly where to begin the hole for the screw inside the first hole and to drill the screw's counterbore deep enough to allow the screw head to clear the bottom of the plug. So try it on some scrap first.

—Jeffrey S. Janssen, Nevada City, Calif.

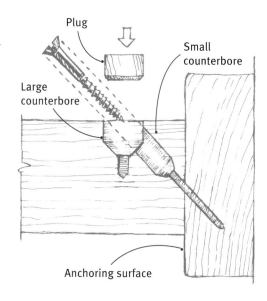

Plug

Small counterbore

Large counterbore

Anchoring surface

Baseboard Shims

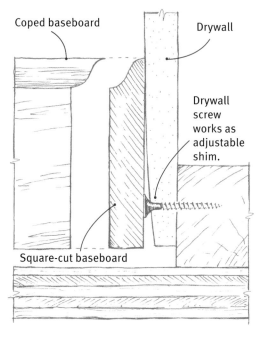

Coped baseboard

Drywall

Drywall screw works as adjustable shim.

Square-cut baseboard

IT CAN BE FRUSTRATING TO INSTALL precisely fit baseboards over an uneven substrate like drywall. Baseboards often sit atop tapered drywall edges, causing the wood to tilt a bit out of plane with the wall. This can cause an unsightly gap at a corner where a coped baseboard intersects a square-cut baseboard, as shown in the drawing at left.

I avoid this problem by driving 1⅛-in. drywall screws into the sill plates at each inside corner. The screws only need to be installed under the square-cut pieces of baseboard. As shown in the drawing, the screws work as adjustable shims, allowing me to run them in or back them out as needed to put the baseboard into plane with the wall. I use a short piece of baseboard with a coped end on it to test the corner joints for fit as I install the square-cut pieces. That way I don't have to keep running back to my saw to adjust the coped cut. For outside corners, I put a screw on each wall.

—Ralph W. Brome, Greensboro, Md.

Little Plugs

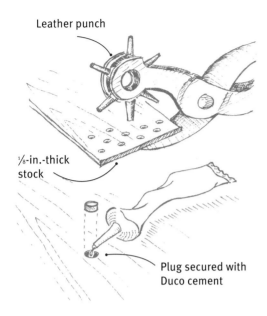

Leather punch

⅛-in.-thick stock

Plug secured with Duco cement

I AM A STAIRBUILDER, and I use thousands of trim screws every year. I countersink the screws into ³⁄₁₆-in.-dia. holes, then fill them with plugs made of the appropriate wood.

However, not one of the wood-shop supply outfits that I deal with has a source for ³⁄₁₆-in. plugs or plug cutters. While researching the subject, it occurred to me that I could use a leather punch to make small-diameter plugs, as shown in the drawing at left. This tool, which looks like a cross between a spur and a pair of pliers, has a rotating wheel full of dies designed to punch holes of varying diameters. I ripped a piece of wood to ⅛ in. thick, and the punch spit out a perfect plug.

When I install the plugs, I first put a dab of Duco brand cement (available at hobby shops) in the hole. Then I wet my finger, pick up a plug with it, insert the plug, and drive it home. I sand it immediately with my palm sander, and I'm ready to move on to the next hole.

—Bob Johnston, Albuquerque, N.M.

Scribing Extension Jambs

FITTING EXTENSION JAMBS to the irregular walls of older homes can be time-consuming. Faced with this task, I get out my veneer saw. First, I rip the extension jambs slightly wider than necessary. Holding a jamb in place with one hand, I slide the saw along the wall so that its teeth scribe a line on the back of the extension jamb, as shown in the drawing at right. A veneer saw's teeth have no set, so they will not mar a finished wall, and the serrated cutting edge is not so apt to wander with the grain the way a knife edge would. Next, I use a plane to trim down to the scribe line at a 3° bevel so that the inside edge of the jamb will stand slightly (and properly) proud of the wall.

—Steve Becker, Valatie, N.Y.

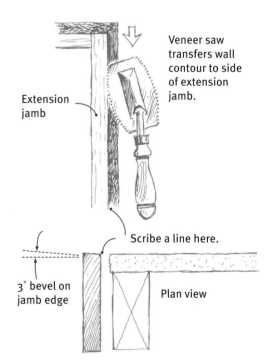

Veneer saw transfers wall contour to side of extension jamb.

Extension jamb

Scribe a line here.

3° bevel on jamb edge

Plan view

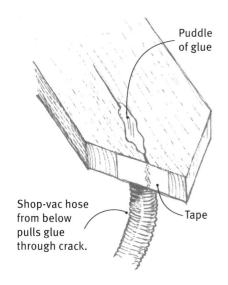

Puddle of glue

Shop-vac hose from below pulls glue through crack.

Tape

Shop Vac Assists Glue-Up

WHILE BUILDING A SET OF STAIRS RECENTLY, I noticed that a crack had developed in the bottom of one of the vertical-grain fir stringers. Because they were exposed on both sides, I wanted to glue and screw the crack closed, but I had difficulty filling the crack with glue.

A coworker's shop vac helped out. As shown in the drawing at left, I poured a little puddle of glue over the top of the crack and applied suction from below. A piece of tape over the end of the crack prevented air from being drawn from the side of the crack. I ran the vacuum until glue began to show up across the bottom of the stringer. It took about 30 seconds to fill a 4-in. crack.

—Gregory Coffin, Loveland, Colo.

Holding Crown Molding

I SOMETIMES WORK ALONE, which means I'm always devising ways of holding up the other end of a board. When it comes to crown molding, I've occasionally used a 10d finish nail to position approximately the far end of the molding while I maneuver the other end into place. This works okay, but not great. Sometimes the molding slips off the nail, and I'm always left with another nail hole to patch.

I solved this problem with the molding cradle that's shown in the drawing at right. The cradle starts with a 24-in. by 6-in. by ½-in. piece of scrap plywood. I affixed a telescoping tent pole to the plywood, using an old push-broom bracket to make the connection. A strip of wood edging along the top of the plywood and a layer of carpet pad were the last touches I added to the cradle. Now I can quickly adjust the cradle up and down depending on the height of the ceiling, and I don't have to worry about damaging the walls. By the way, I'm sure a painter's telescoping roller handle would work just as well as my tent pole.

—Charles T. O'Neill, Cranford, N.J.

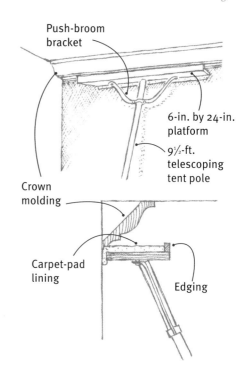

Push-broom bracket

6-in. by 24-in. platform

9½-ft. telescoping tent pole

Crown molding

Carpet-pad lining

Edging

Router-Made Moldings

I NEEDED A SPECIAL MOLDING to complete a baseboard detail, but my router table was several hundred miles away on another job. Fortunately, the situation forced me to come up with an alternative method for site-milling trim stock. I think my new method is faster, more accurate, and safer than using a router table—especially if the moldings are narrow and thin.

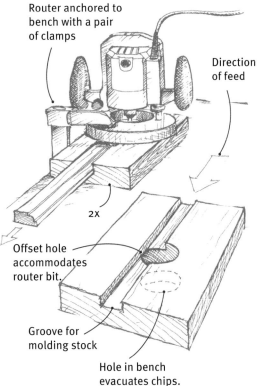

Router anchored to bench with a pair of clamps

Direction of feed

2x

Offset hole accommodates router bit.

Groove for molding stock

Hole in bench evacuates chips.

As shown in the drawing at right, I used a scrap of 2x stock about 1 ft. long and about the width of my router's base. I cut a lengthwise groove near the middle of the 2x, just a pinch larger than the depth and width of my molding stock. Then I used a hole saw to bore a 1½-in.-dia. hole that is offset from the center of the groove. This hole accommodates the router bit, and it should be to the left of the groove as you face the jig. This is to ensure that the router bit, which turns clockwise, will be turning into the work as you feed the stock into it. Next, I bored a similar hole in the top of my job-site workbench to allow the wood chips an escape route.

I positioned my router over the hole in the jig and anchored the router to the table with a pair of clamps. The clamps were arranged on opposite sides of the router's base in line down the groove. I could easily adjust the router, both vertically and horizontally, until I had the bit in the exact position that I needed for the molding profile. Cutting the moldings is a simple matter of turning on the router and feeding the stock into the groove. In a few minutes I had hundreds of feet of molding. And because the stock was captured in the groove of the jig under the base of the router, my fingers never got near the cutters.

—Bill Young, Berkeley, Calif.

Sandpaper Grip

WHEN SANDING A ROUNDED FORM, such as a handrail, finger sanding gives you the best feel for the shape of the work. For a better grip on your sandpaper, use double-sided adhesive tape on the back of the paper. This will keep your hand and the sandpaper moving at the same speed.

—Jeff McDermott, Phoenix, Ariz.

Ripping Plastic Laminate

WHENEVER I HAVE TO MAKE LONG, NARROW STRIPS of plastic laminate, I start by putting my portable saw on the floor. That way the floor can act as a huge saw table to support the floppy ends of the laminate as it's passed over the blade. As shown in the drawing at right, I mounted a pair of wooden hold-downs on my saw's fence to keep the laminate from riding up as it's cut.

I wrapped the metal fence that came with the saw with a piece of ¾-in. plywood. The plywood serves as a base for the screws that secure the hold-down brackets. And unlike the saw's factory-issue fence, the bottom edge of my modified fence meets the saw table, which prevents the thin plastic from sliding under the fence.

This system works best when you've got two people to manage the unruly sheets. But I've also used the rig solo to rip narrow strips from a 4-ft. by 12-ft. sheet of plastic laminate.

—Byron Papa, Madison, Ala.

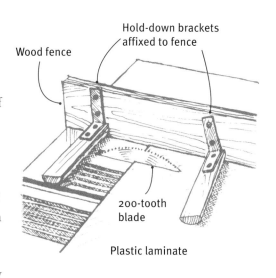

Wood fence

Hold-down brackets affixed to fence

200-tooth blade

Plastic laminate

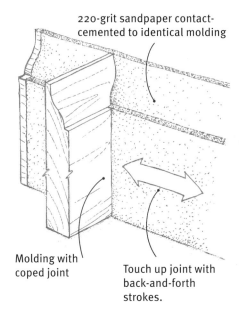

220-grit sandpaper contact-cemented to identical molding

Molding with coped joint

Touch up joint with back-and-forth strokes.

Touching Up Coped Joints

THE DRAWING AT LEFT SHOWS A TRICK THAT I TEACH MY STUDENTS for making perfect coped joints. We use water-based contact cement to glue a sheet of 220-grit sandpaper to a piece of molding that has the same profile as the workpiece. Result: a custom-made, contoured sanding block. Using the block to make a few back-and-forth strokes on the coped end of the workpiece will smooth out unsightly irregularities.

—David Johnson, Clinton, Iowa

Baseboard Corner Blocks

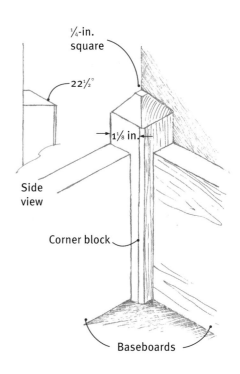

THE DRAWING AT RIGHT SHOWS A DETAIL we use to craft an attractive, simple inside-corner detail for baseboards. With this detail, gaps in inside corners are a thing of the past. We typically install oiled 1x4 hemlock baseboards in our houses, so we use 1⅛-in.-sq. stock for the corner blocks. The extra thickness leaves a nice reveal where the base intersects the block and hides inconsistencies in thickness.

To make the blocks, we first bevel the front edge of a long piece of stock with a power planer. Then we use a chopsaw to cut two 22½° bevels. As shown in the drawing, we leave a ¼-in. by ¼-in. flat atop each block. Then we cut the block to length (usually 3¾ in.).

We nail the block from behind to one of the pieces of baseboard before installation. And because the blocks provide a flat, vertical surface, it's easy to get accurate measurements from block to block.

—Tibor Breuer, Olympia, Wash.

¼-in. square

22½°

1⅛ in.

Side view

Corner block

Baseboards

Another Way to Glue Backsplashes

I USED TO USE BRACES to hold a backsplash in place while the construction adhesive set up. But it's a pain to install the braces, and furthermore, you have to go back the next day to remove them and to finish the job by caulking the joints.

Now, instead of using braces, I break out my hot-glue gun. The first part of the process remains identical. I cut the backsplashes and adjust them to fit as needed. Then I apply the construction adhesive to the back of the splash. Now the trick. I put dime-size blobs of hot glue, spaced 2 ft. to 3 ft. apart, on the back of the splash. I then put the splash in place and hold it firmly to the wall for about a minute while the hot glue sets up. The hot glue will hold the backsplash in place while the construction adhesive cures. Meanwhile, I can immediately apply the caulk, finishing up the job without having to go back the next day.

—Robert T. Alexander, Virginia Beach, Va.

Hot-melt glue

Backsplash

Counter

Construction adhesive

Kerf Block Speeds the Sawcuts

I OFTEN FIND IT EASIER, especially doing built-in units on site, to bring some hand-held power tools to the lumber and plywood pile rather than haul the material back to the shop. I use a circular saw to make my cuts, and with the help of a kerf block, I can make the cuts quickly with accuracy that's around plus or minus 1/16 in. What s a kerf block? Read on.

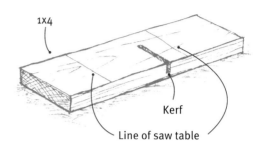

1x4

Kerf

Line of saw table

First, I set the depth of cut on my circular saw. Once it's set, I don't change it, or I'll have to make another kerf block. Next, I grab a scrap piece of wood. A 1-ft.-long piece of 1x4 is good for this process. Now, using my square, I start cutting across the block. I stop the cut midway, and with the saw stuck in the wood, I use a sharp pencil to mark the edges of the saw's table on both sides of the cut. The block should look like the drawing at right.

Now when I want to make a cut in a sheet of plywood, I mark the dimension on the plywood and hold the block on the work so that the kerf lines up with the mark. Then I note the edge of the saw table (whichever side is most convenient) with a pencil mark on the plywood. I use these marks to position a clamped-on straightedge to guide my circular saw. This method works equally well when dadoing with a router.

—Randall C. Smith, Barrington, N.H.

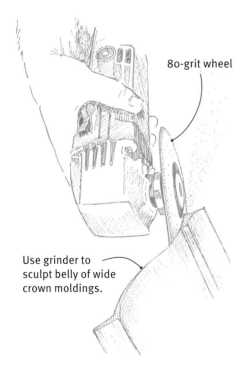

80-grit wheel

Use grinder to sculpt belly of wide crown moldings.

Coping with a Grinder

I'M A TRIM CARPENTER who prefers to cope crown molding rather than cut inside miters. I use a variety of tools to shape the cuts, and one of my favorites is my little Makita grinder. With an 80-grit wheel, I can back-cut a piece of crown with speed and accuracy. This is especially important when sculpting the belly, or the big central curve, as shown in the drawing at left. I also use my grinder for fine scribe cuts on cabinets, doors, and trim. It's the perfect tool for a situation where I don't have good control with my belt sander.

—Chris Solberg, Corte Madera, Calif.

Coping with Rounded Trim

OUR CLIENT'S HOUSE HAS SOME ARCHED WINDOWS and doorways, and to remain in keeping with these openings the trim pieces have edges that have been radiused with a ⅜-in. round-over bit. The rounded trim adds a nice touch, but when it came time to attractively join chair rails and baseboards with the door trim, we found ourselves with a problem to solve. My partner, Paul Hannenmann, came up with the solution shown in the drawings at right.

First he made an adjustable fence out of a piece of ¼-in. acrylic for his Porter-Cable laminate trimmer. The fence has slots in it that allow it to be moved in relation to the bit. The screws provided on the tool's base hold the fence in place. Using a ½-in. core box bit, Paul plowed a radiused groove in the end of a piece of 1x pine trim, as shown in the top drawing at right. He adjusted the fence to leave a paper-thin edge on the exposed side of the trim. Then he used a table saw to remove the back edge of the groove, as shown in the center drawing at right. The finished reverse curve allows the base or chair-rail member to abut the door casing without a gap, as shown in the bottom drawing at right.

—Anthony Patillo, Conway, Mass.

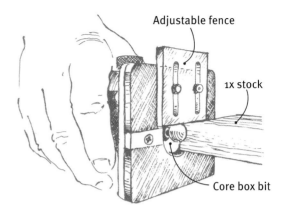

Make radiused groove with laminate trimmer.

Remove back edge with the table saw.

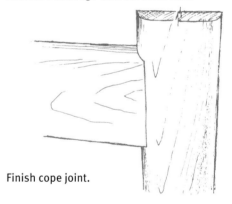

Finish cope joint.

Measuring Casing Legs

WHENEVER I TRIM OUT A DOOR OR A WINDOW, I first attach the head casing, cut to the finished length. Then I make the miter cut on each leg (side casing) and check the miters for fit. At this point each leg is still about ½ in. too long. Instead of trying to measure the exact length, I turn the trim upside down, with the point of the miter resting on the floor (or window stool). Making sure the trim is lined up with my reveal marks, I strike a line on the trim even with the top of the head casing. Then I cut the leg square, leaving the line, and the trim fits tightly every time.

—Patrick D. Rabbitt, Greenwich, Conn.

Supporting a Sink Cutout

I'VE FOUND THE MOST EFFECTIVE WAY TO SUPPORT A SINK cutout is to make the cut a little more than halfway around the sink outline. Then I affix a strip of scrap wood to the cutout with a single screw in the middle. The scrap should be long enough to overlap the cut at both ends. Now I can complete the cut with both hands on the saw as the scrap supports the waste piece.

—Allan Smith, via e-mail

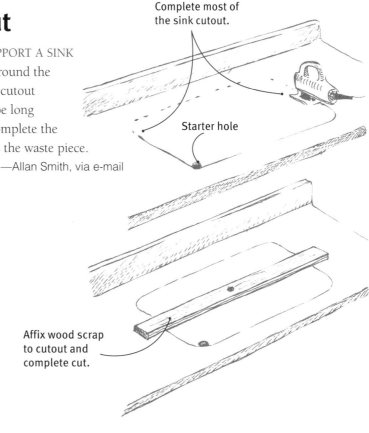

Complete most of the sink cutout.

Starter hole

Affix wood scrap to cutout and complete cut.

Coping Quarter Round

THE DRAWING AT RIGHT SHOWS THE METHOD I use to cope the end of a piece of quarter-round molding. Using this trick, I can quickly and accurately make coped inside corners, such as the intersection of quarter-round toe molding at the bottom of a baseboard.

As shown in the drawing, I use a Forstner bit that is twice the radius of the molding to cut the cope. For example, a ¾-in. quarter round requires a 1½-in. bit. To make sure the edge of the molding is centered under the axis of the bit, I hold the molding against an auxiliary fence mounted on my drill press.

—Herb Alberry, Odessa, Ontario

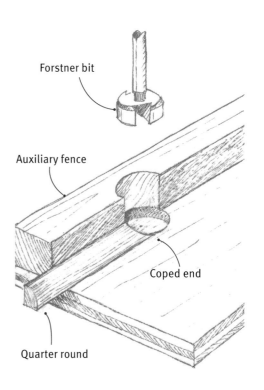

Forstner bit

Auxiliary fence

Coped end

Quarter round

Patching a Hardwood Strip Floor

To make a convincing patch in a hardwood strip floor, you've got to stagger the ends of the adjacent strips. Otherwise, the patch will look like a poorly concealed trap door. The problem is, how do you accurately and efficiently make numerous cuts in hardwood strips while they are already in place? The drawing at right shows how I recently solved this dilemma. The tools required are a plunge router with a ¼-in. or ⅜-in. straight bit, a circular saw with a nail-cutting carbide blade, safety glasses and a face shield, a chisel, and a nail-finder (you can use either the swinging-magnetic kind, or one of the coil types powered by a battery).

First, find out which edge of the strips have the tongues, and therefore the nails. If you're working from a visible end, this will be obvious. Otherwise, find a spot in the middle of the patch that doesn't have any nearby nails, make a couple of cuts across a strip, and pry it out. Next, run the nail finder down the edge of each strip and mark the locations of the nails. Now you can lay out a series of staggered cut lines for the new strips that avoid any nails. To sever the nails, make plunge cuts on the waste side of the strip flooring—be sure to wear the safety goggles and face shield during this operation.

I used my router, guided by a strip of wood, to make perpendicular cuts across the strips. The width of the cut gave me enough room to get the end of the prybar under the strip that needs to be pulled up. At this point, a chisel is sometimes handy for splitting the tongue off a strip that is reluctant to come out. I also use the chisel to square the ends of the slots. Chamfering the leading bottom corners and edge (plus a little patience) will help as you insert the replacement strips.

—Ted Garner, Chicago, Ill.

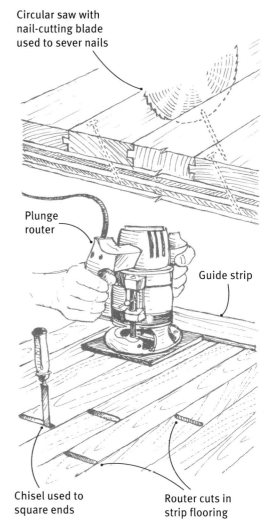

Circular saw with nail-cutting blade used to sever nails

Plunge router

Guide strip

Chisel used to square ends

Router cuts in strip flooring

Laminate Spacer

On a recent kitchen remodel I found myself ready to attach the plastic laminate to the countertop with contact cement, but I didn't have my usual stack of spacers that I use to separate the counter and laminate during alignment. In need of a handy alternative, I turned to a thin extension cord in my kit. I found that by looping the cord across the counter, as shown, I could position the laminate, then remove the cord starting with the loop nearest the center of the counter.

—Hayes Rutherford, Coolin, Idaho

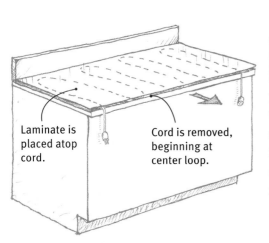

Laminate is placed atop cord.

Cord is removed, beginning at center loop.

Coping Quarter-Round Trim

I RECENTLY HAD TO INSTALL a lot of ¾-in. quarter-round trim. I prefer coped corners to mitered corners, but given the amount of trim required by this job, I had to find an expedient way to cut the stuff. As shown in the drawing at right, I devised a fixture that yields accurate results with a minimum of effort.

I started with a scrap piece of 2x6 about 14 in. long. Using my table saw, I plowed a ¾-in. by ¾-in. groove the length of the 2x6 to accommodate the quarter-round trim. This groove holds the trim as it is cut by a 1½-in.-dia. hole saw from above. As shown in the drawing, the hole saw is guided by a 1x4 guide block. I made this block out of oak because it holds up well after repetitive cuts.

Using this rig makes coping quarter-round trim a breeze. For quarter-rounds of a different radius, simply cut a groove to fit the trim and use a hole saw that is twice the radius of the trim.

—M. P. Whipple, Afton, N.Y.

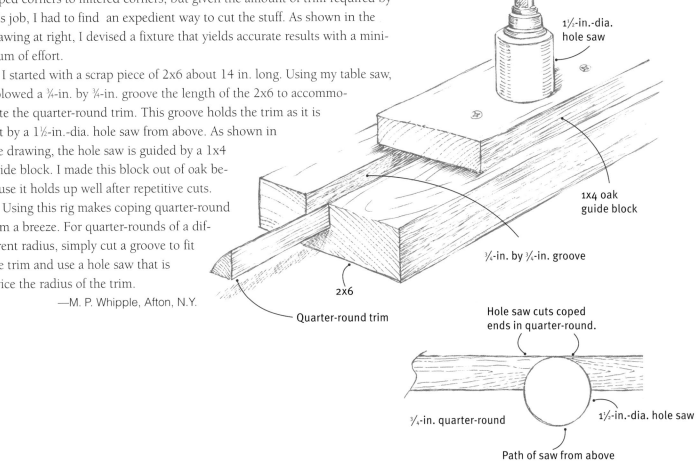

1½-in.-dia. hole saw

1x4 oak guide block

¾-in. by ¾-in. groove

2x6

Quarter-round trim

Hole saw cuts coped ends in quarter-round.

¾-in. quarter-round

1½-in.-dia. hole saw

Path of saw from above

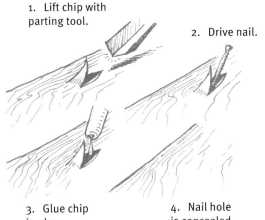

1. Lift chip with parting tool.

2. Drive nail.

3. Glue chip in place.

4. Nail hole is concealed.

Invisible Nailing

WE DON'T WORRY ABOUT FILLING NAIL HOLES—we eliminate them. Before driving the nail, we use a gouge or a parting tool to lift a small chip of wood from the surface of the work (1 in the drawing). Be careful not to break off the chip. Now drive the nail into the resulting groove (2), and countersink it. Glue the chip back in place (3), and you've got a concealed nail hole with perfectly matching grain (4).

—Daniel Casciato and Christopher Gecik, Cleveland, Ohio

13
Painting & Caulking

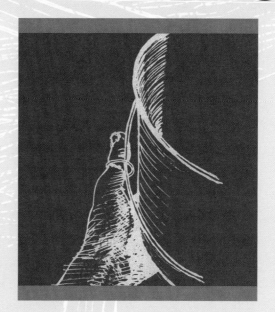

Paintbrush Carrier

WHEN I PAINT TRIMWORK, I hate to waste time climbing up and down the ladder to get the right brush. I could leave my various brushes in my paint bucket, but they would soon become a dripping mess.

My solution is to cut the top off a one-gallon plastic antifreeze jug with flat sides. I then cut two slits in one of the sides and thread a nylon belt through them, as shown in the drawing at right. I slide the loose belt ends through the loops of my painter's pants, creating a paintbrush carrier that rides easily on my hip. I now have several brushes close at hand. The carrier cleans up easily with water or paint thinner.

—Mike Ellis, Seattle, Wash.

Scraper Cleanup

PAINT STRIPPER COMBINED WITH old paint or varnish makes a sticky goo that can be tough to remove from a scraper or a putty knife. To make an easy job of it, I cut a straight slit about 2 in. long in a large tin can. Then I slide the blade of the knife into the slit close to where it joins the handle. When I pull the blade out, the old finish falls into the can, ready for disposal.

—Roy Viken, Boise, Idaho

Stain Control

IF YOU'VE GOT A WOOD-STAINING JOB coming up, consider using a pad painter to apply the stain with. The foam pad holds more stain than a brush, and the flow can be controlled by the amount of pressure that you apply. I have found that with a little practice, I can almost eliminate the need for wiping the stain with a rag.

I use an old plastic dishwashing-soap bottle to deliver stain to the pad. It has a pop-up cap so it's easy to close, thereby eliminating the chance of a major spill. To keep the stain "stirred," I shake the bottle now and then.

—Emily Neal, Alfred Station, N.Y.

Caulking-Gun Care

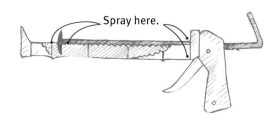

Spray here.

MY CAULKING GUNS used to accumulate gobs of hardened caulk and mastic on the plunger, making cartridge removal very difficult. The tough rubbery mass (silicone is the worst) was a real nuisance and prompted the early retirement of several guns. Then I discovered the trick of spraying some silicone lubricant (WD-40 works too) on the plunger and into the back of the barrel. The lubrication lets the encrustations peel off in one piece and makes changing tubes easy. You'll have to renew this lubricant every so often. One warning, though: If your gun has a friction-type drive mechanism, don't spray it—the lubrication will render it useless.

—William H. Brennen, Denver, Colo.

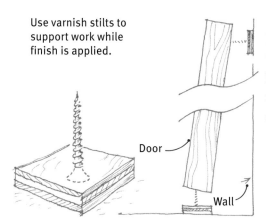

Use varnish stilts to support work while finish is applied.

Door

Wall

Paint Stilts

A DRYWALL SCREW THROUGH A SMALL SQUARE of plywood makes a handy stilt to prop up work while finish is applied. When I paint a door, for instance, I place a pair of stilts on the floor to support the door and another one against the wall near the top of the door, as shown at left.

—Michael R. Sweem, Downey, Calif.

Spud Fingers

IF YOU ARE CAULKING A JOINT and running out of clean fingers to smooth the caulk with, try using a potato. Before a job, I carve spuds to the desired profile and store them in a plastic bag. I've found that the acidic potato juice keeps silicone and other caulking materials from sticking to the spud fingers.

—Glen Zahn, Fairbanks, Alaska

Centrifugal Roller Cleaner

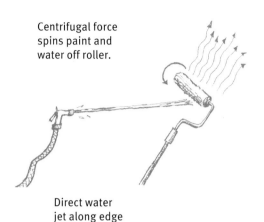

Centrifugal force spins paint and water off roller.

Direct water jet along edge of roller.

CLEANING WATER-SOLUBLE PAINT from a paint roller used to be a tedious chore until I came up with this idea. Now after the painting is finished, I simply attach an extension handle to the roller, step outside, and use a garden hose to do the work. By directing a water stream along the edge of the roller, the roller revs up to a good speed and spins the paint and water off the roller, as shown in the drawing at left. Be sure that you perform this operation away from anything that might be damaged by the paint and water overspray.

—Mel Wolpert, Weatogue, Conn.

Help for Spray-Can Nozzles

I WANTED TO USE A PARTIALLY CONSUMED can of spray paint the other day, but the perennial problem prevented me from doing so—the nozzle was full of dried-up paint. I searched around the shop for another nozzle and ended up using the one off my can of WD-40. When I put the nozzle back on the can of WD-40, I gave it a squirt to clean it out, and realized that I can do the same thing with my spray-can nozzles. Now when I'm done using a can of spray paint, I put its nozzle on the WD-40 can for a cleansing blast.

—Charles Buell, Washington, Maine

Perpetual Paintbrushes

WHEN USING OIL PAINTS, I don't enjoy cleaning the brush at the end of the day, only to get it dirty again the next morning. So between uses, I simply stick the brush in a can of water.

The water keeps the air away, and thus keeps the brush from setting up. This works for varnish, stain, and oils as well. When I'm ready to use the brush, I just give it a few heavy strokes against a clean cardboard box. Oil and water don't normally mix, so what little water remains on the bristles is rapidly absorbed into the cardboard.

—Mark White, Kodiak, Alaska

Caulk Tube Cap

THERE ARE A LOT OF NEW CAULKS AND ADHESIVES available in tubes these days. I've found uses for many of them, but I rarely finish a tube on one job. In fact, many tasks need only a little squirt of some high-priced goo. Leftover tubes might just as well be tossed into the trash on the spot because the material in the top becomes hard and unusable, rendering the rest of the contents inaccessible. A versatile and effective cap would solve the problem—and I had some in my toolbox all along.

The solution is wire nuts. I use vinyl-coated red ones, which are normally used on 12-ga. wire, to cap my unspent tubes. I've found them effective for up to six months, and they can be constantly reused and easily replaced.

—Joe Shepherd, Milwaukie, Ore.

1x1 curb

3 ft.

Plastic blade

Offset casters

Paint Caddy

I PAINT HOUSES FOR A LIVING, and there are three things about painting with a roller that really annoy me. One is masking the baseboard and spreading out a tarp to catch drips and speckles. Another is moving the paint bucket from station to station, and the third is moving the tarp again, which inevitably results in drops of wet paint smearing the carpet or floor.

Instead of this sequence, I now use a plywood platform on wheels both to carry the paint bucket and to protect the baseboard and floor from paint splatters. A plastic blade on one end of the platform butts up against the wall to catch drips, as shown in the drawing at at left. To make the blade, I used a section cut out of an old plastic garbage can, and I attached it to the caddy so the curve points upward. This directs paint away from the wall, and accommodates the higher baseboards.

—Stan Lucas, Redmond, Wash.

Wood Filler

I'VE FOUND THAT BONDO and other auto-body fillers like it make excellent wood fillers for exterior and interior painted surfaces. They adhere to wood better than most wood fillers. They don't shrink. They saw, drill, and plane better than typical wood fillers. And best of all, auto-body fillers set up in just 30 minutes, no matter how large the cavity you are filling.

—Jim Stuart, Covina, Calif.

Wiping Paint Brushes

PAINTERS OFTEN TAKE THE EXCESS PAINT off their brushes by wiping the sides of the bristles on the inside lip of the can. Eventually the channel around the rim fills up, and paint runs down the outside of the can. Some painters avoid this problem by poking holes in the bottom of the channel with a 16d nail, the theory being that the paint will drip back into the can before filling the channel to overflowing. My solution to this problem avoids the rim altogether.

As shown in the photo at left, I bend a stiff piece of wire (like a coat hanger) into a crossbar that spans the can. The wire hangs on the rim of the can a little off center to make the paint easy to reach with my brush. I wipe the excess paint on the wire, and the paint simply drips back into the can without touching the rim. The crossbar is easily removed for cleaning and reuse. If I'm using a paper or plastic container, I poke holes in the sides near the top and run a straight wire through them.

—Michael R. Hogan, St. Croix, V.I.

Stack Painting

WHEN YOU'VE GOT TO BRUSH PAINT OR STAIN on the edges of many boards, try stacking them flat so that you can apply the finish to all of them at once. This will save you a tremendous amount of time compared to treating each edge separately. When you've got them all coated, slightly stagger the pile and brush out any excess finish that may be on the faces and backs of the boards.

—Ed Kobus, Spring, Md.

Stack boards to paint edges. Stagger them to brush out excess finish.

Foiling Paint Drips

TO PROTECT ITEMS SUCH AS HINGES, doorknobs, or wall phones when I'm painting, I simply wrap them with aluminum foil. It can be molded quickly to fit even the oddest shapes, and it stays put while I wield the brush. It also applies faster and removes easier than tape.

—Marie Christopher, Brady, Tex.

Shelf Drying Rack

THE NEXT TIME YOU HAVE A STACK OF SHELVES or cabinet doors to paint, don't lean them against the wall. Instead, try hanging them from a rope that has been stretched clothesline style. As shown in the drawing below, the line is knotted every 6 in. to 8 in. These knots create hitching posts for the cup hooks that I screw into the edge of each shelf.

—Bruce Schwarz, Manchester, Md.

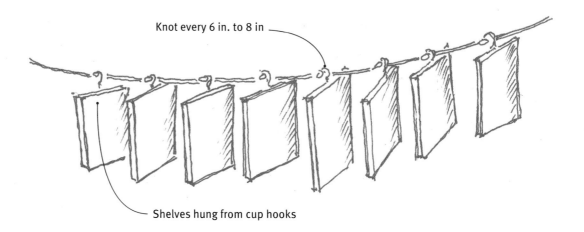

Knot every 6 in. to 8 in

Shelves hung from cup hooks

Painted-Trim Prep

SOMETIMES WHEN A HOUSE INTERIOR NEEDS REPAINTING, the woodwork is too rough to take a new coat of paint, but not bad enough to warrant stripping. Under these circumstances, I prepare the woodwork by using a sponge, a bucket of water, a scrub brush, and some wet/dry sandpaper. I keep the sandpaper and work surface wet throughout the process, and I use my hands or the sponge as a sanding pad. I find that the paper will last up to an hour if I periodically use the brush to scrub the paper in the bucket.

Using this wet process keeps the dust suspended in the water rather than in the air. The resulting surface is quite smooth to the touch, but it still has the necessary roughness for good paint adhesion. I've used this technique with old oil-base and water-base paints with equally good results.

—John Glenn, Brookline, Mass.

An Efficient Way to Paint Doors

HERE'S A SIMPLE WAY to take some of the frustration out of painting doors. As shown in the drawing at right, I drive a couple of nails into the top and bottom of the door (you could also use 3-in. drywall screws) and suspend the door between a couple of sawhorses. Once I've got one side finished, it's an easy matter to pivot the door 180° and then paint its other side. And because the nail holes are on the top and bottom of the doors, they're out of sight.

—Charles P. McCausland, Hall, N.Y.

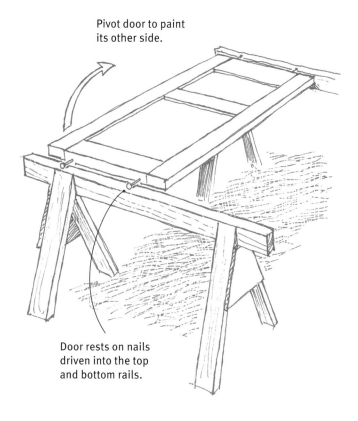

Pivot door to paint its other side.

Door rests on nails driven into the top and bottom rails.

Steady That Bucket

ATTACHING A 1¼-IN. SPLIT-SPIRAL KEY RING to the bail of your paint pot makes holding a bucket all day a lot easier. Support the bottom of the bucket with your hand, as shown in the photo below, and slip your thumb through the ring to steady it.

—Bryan Humphrey, Wilmington, N.C.

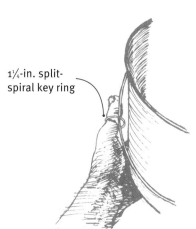

1¼-in. split-spiral key ring

Drying Rack

WE PREPRIME AND VARNISH a lot of the trim we install in houses, and finding a good place to let the material dry without getting in the way used to be difficult. To solve the problem I came up with the drying rack shown in the drawing at right. I make the brackets out of standard 2x dimension lumber. Using a drill press, I drill 1-in.-dia. holes 6 in. apart for 3-ft.-long, 1-in. dowels. As shown in the drawing, the brackets lean against the wall at a 20° angle, and the holes are oriented at a 70° angle so that the dowels end up level while the racks are in use.

I space the racks about 6 ft. apart and start loading them from the bottom up. It's amazing how much material they will hold and how strong they are. I've even used them to hold freshly painted doors.

—Daniel E. Perry, Vineyard Haven, Mass.

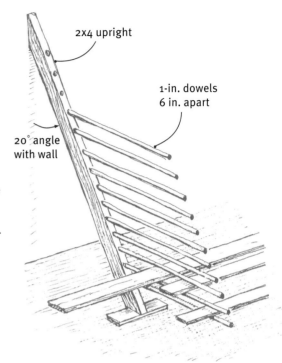

2x4 upright

1-in. dowels
6 in. apart

20° angle
with wall

Tarps for Pressure-Washing

PRESSURE-WASHING FLAKING PAINT OFF SIDING can leave millions of unsightly paint chips strewn around a building. There's no good way to pick up any but the largest pieces. One client was adamant that he didn't want any chips around his home. I planned to lay down tarps to collect the chips when we hand-scraped, but the tarps would be flooded by the water during the preliminary wash. To catch the flakes and let the water pass through, I spread some landscaping fabric left over from another project about 6 ft. out from the house. Although the water puddled up initially, it passed through shortly after we shut off the equipment, and it caught even the tiniest particles.

—Mike Guertin, East Greenwich, R.I.

Caulking in Tight Spots

A PIECE OF PLASTIC SHEATHING from a 12- or 14-ga. wiring cable (such as Romex) makes an effective caulking-tube extension when the tube's nozzle doesn't have the flex to reach the spot in need.

—Macolm McDaniel, Berkeley, Calif.

Milk-Jug Paint Pot

1-gal. milk jug

DURING OUR EPISODIC REMODELING PROJECTS, it occasionally comes time for me to get out the paint or varnish. For these jobs I use a special, user-friendly paint pot made from a 1-gal. plastic milk jug. As shown in the drawing at left, I cut a window in the front of the jug.

I think this paint pot has several advantages. The handle is rigidly attached, making it less likely to cause a spill. The edge lets me wipe off the brush with no paint-can grooves to fill up and overflow, and the hole at the top provides a convenient place to put the brush when I need a free hand. But best of all, the vertical handle keeps my wrist at a comfortable angle. Ergonomics at no cost whatsoever.

—Walter Alvarez, Berkeley, Calif.

A Use for Expired Credit Cards

RATHER THAN RELY ON MY FINGERS for tooling fresh caulk, I use old credit cards. Their rounded corners leave a perfect radius. I can even vary the radius by changing the angle of the card as I draw it along the corner. And if I need a sharper corner, I can trim the card to fit with some snips.

—Richard Woolfort, St. Charles, Mo.

14

Electric
& Plumbing

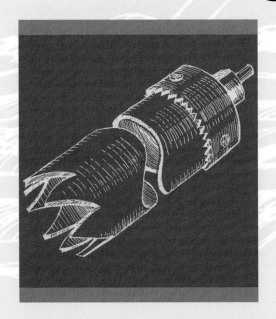

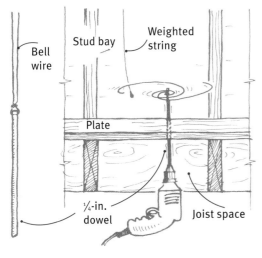

Bell wire

Stud bay

Weighted string

Plate

¼-in. dowel

Joist space

Rotary Fishing Rod

WHEN FISHING A WIRE FOR A DOORBELL RECENTLY, I ran into a seemingly impossible situation. I'd drilled the hole for the bell-push and an angled hole through the wall plate into the proper stud bay from the cellar. But try as I might, I couldn't get a wire from one to the other. I tried fish tape, a weighted string, bell wire, bead chain, profanity, hooks, probes, and a dozen other ploys. I couldn't find any obstruction, but couldn't find the wire, either.

As my last attempt before starting to rip clapboards off the side of the house, I made the "fishing rod" shown in the drawing. Starting with a piece of ¼-in. dowel about a foot long, I drilled a 1/16-in. hole across the diameter about ⅛ in. from one end. Through this hole I inserted a 15-in. piece of bell wire that I secured with a square knot, leaving the two ends equal.

I then chucked the other end of the dowel in an electric drill. Folding the ends of the wire so they stuck out ahead of the dowel like antennae, I shoved the contraption into the hole in the plate as far as it would go and turned on the drill. At 1,200 rpm, the ends of the wire whipped out centrifugally, lashing around inside the wall and almost immediately entangling the weighted string left dangling from the bell-push hole. When I pulled the drill back through the hole in the plate, I found the string securely wrapped around the dowel.

—Robert L. Edsall, New Haven, Conn.

On-Site Bender

NOTHING IS WORSE THAN showing up at a job to discover that an important tool didn't make it into the truck. One day, I left my conduit bender at home, so I used scrap wood to make a bender that gave me beautiful, kink-free bends in my ½-in. conduit.

I started with a piece of 2x8 about 15 in. long for the body, and I attached a short piece of 1x4 to it with screws to act as a stop. Next I cut a 90° arc into the end of a 5-ft. 2x6 and nailed it to the body as shown at right. Since most of the 2x6 needed to act as a handle, I tapered its width to about 3 in. to make the tool less cumbersome, and I was back in business.

—Richard Tufts, Santa Rosa, Calif.

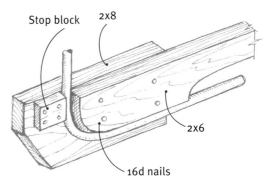

Stop block

2x8

2x6

16d nails

Pipe Soldering Blast Shield

ONE EVENING LAST SPRING, I was sweating together some copper water lines in my unfinished house. As my acetylene flame scorched a joist, I realized that I needed to find a heat shield so that I wouldn't burn down the house. It was late enough that a Home Depot run would have finished me off for the night, so I cast about for a substitute for a commercial heat shield. Lighting onto some scraps of fibercement siding, I knew I'd found a winner. Composed largely of concrete, I was sure that the fibercement wouldn't burn. I jigsawed a slot into a scrap so that I could slide it over the pipe near any framing, and went on sweating.

—Andy Engel, Roxbury, Conn.

Getting a Line on Setting a Toilet

SETTING A TOILET SINGLE-HANDEDLY presents a tricky problem: If you don't accurately line up the closet bolts with the holes in the base of the toilet bowl, you can damage the wax ring that seals the toilet to its flange. The drawing at left shows my solution to the dilemma.

I take a couple of inches of stiff wire and wrap it around the end of each closet bolt. This leaves a couple of wire feelers sticking up to act as guides, ensuring that the bowl is lined up correctly before the wax ring makes contact with the closet flange.

—R. B. Himes, Vienna, Ohio

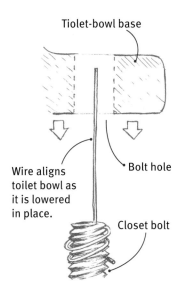

Tiolet-bowl base

Bolt hole

Wire aligns toilet bowl as it is lowered in place.

Closet bolt

Nail Plates in a Pinch

ON A RECENT REMODELING JOB I needed a couple of the metal safety plates that are used to shield plumbing and wiring from drywall nails. In my bucket of parts that are too good to throw away, I found just what I needed: side plates from the kind of metal outlet boxes that can be ganged together. The plates are even predrilled for nails or screws.

—Roger S. Apted, Milton, Wis.

Wiring in Old Walls

HERE ARE SOME TRICKS to help you use a fish tape when you're trying to run new wiring through old walls. A fish tape is a thin, spring-steel wire with a hook on one end. It's mounted on a spool and most often used to pull wiring through sections of conduit. It can also snake through hidden wall and ceiling cavities.

It can be hard to hit a target with a fish tape. So I catch it with a string. When you're working on a vertical run, such as an attic to a wall-mounted outlet, lower the string from above. It should be tied into a series of loops, one pushed through the other, and the string weighted with a piece of solder. The fish tape is then introduced into the lower access hold and manipulated until its hook catches one of the loops. The same trick can work horizontally—push the weighted string along the flat run with a stick until it falls into the vertical cavity.

Another way to get a string from one place to another in an empty conduit is to tie it around a small wad of cellophane and use compressed air to blow it down the run. Then tie it to a heavier string, and you're ready to haul on the tape. For a really convoluted run, where a normal fish tape won't follow the necessary path, a speedometer cable can do the job. When you are doing this kind of work, make sure that you know the location of any live boxes and unprotected wiring, like knob and tube work. And to make things easier in the event of future wiring changes, leave a piece of nylon string pulled through the runs.

—Norman Rabek, Burnsville, N.C.

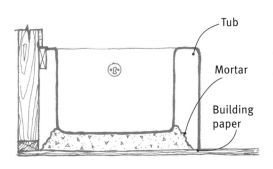

Tub

Mortar

Building paper

Tub Support

IF YOU ARE ABOUT TO INSTALL a lightweight steel or fiberglass tub, here's a way to make it feel more substantial. Set it on a bed—or rather a blob—of mortar.

First staple building felt to the subfloor in the area to be occupied by the tub. Spread a thick, stiff blanket of mortar onto the felt so that it will cradle the bathtub, as shown in the drawing at left. What was once a flimsy tub bottom with no thermal mass is now solid as a rock and able to retain warmth. It's a very nice touch if you can't use cast iron.

—Kurt Lavenson, Berkeley, Calif.

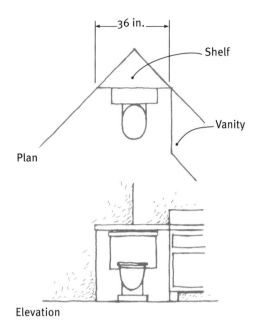

36 in.

Shelf

Vanity

Plan

Elevation

The Bathroom Angle

THE DRAWING AT LEFT ILLUSTRATES an idea that I use frequently in the houses that I design. It revolves around mounting the toilet at a 45° angle in the bathroom corner. Positioned this way, the toilet looks better, it s easier to clean around, and there is room behind it for a convenient shelf.

These were some of the bonus features of the design. My original intention was just to make it more convenient for folks in wheelchairs. Many have to face the toilet to get on it…me for instance.

—Jay Wallace, Ashland, Ore.

Shower-Stall Backing

HERE'S AN INEXPENSIVE WAY to make the thin, flimsy walls of a fiberglass shower more rigid. Apply expanding urethane foam at several spots up and down the wall studs behind the shower walls, as shown in the drawing at right. The foam will do its expanding sideways. When it cures, the shower walls will have a lot less give.

—Byron Papa, Schriever, La.

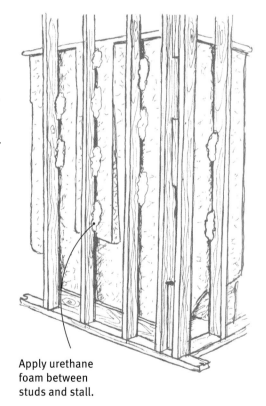

Apply urethane foam between studs and stall.

Drilling Holes in EPS

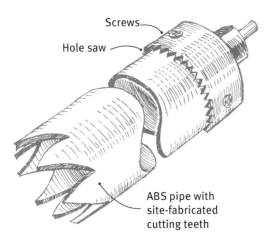

Screws

Hole saw

ABS pipe with site-fabricated cutting teeth

I NEEDED TO DRILL AN 8-FT.-LONG HOLE in the EPS core of a stress-skin panel in order to install a vent pipe for a kitchen sink. I don't know of any off-the-shelf bits or hole saws that are designed for a task like this, so I made my own, using a piece of the same pipe that would end up in the hole. I used my coping saw to cut teeth in the end of a piece of ABS pipe. A coworker improved my design by using a Sure-form plane to sharpen the teeth.

As shown in the drawing at left, I mounted the other end of the 2-in. pipe in a 2⅜-in.-dia. hole saw. It fit perfectly. Three drywall screws through the slots in the side of the hole saw secured the ABS. Presto! I had a hole saw 8 ft. long attached to my ½-in. Hole Hawg drill. It easily cut a hole in the foam that was the exact size I needed.

—Jim Frandeen, Soquel, Calif.

Electrician's Carryall

AN ELECTRICIAN HAS TO CARRY a bewildering array of fasteners and other tiny components, and keeping them organized and close at hand can be frustrating. For me, the perfect way to carry these supplies is with a fly-fisherman's vest. Mine is a multipocketed affair that has touch-fastener pocket flaps. It has served me well for years, and it is comfortable enough to let me work in crawl spaces and on ladders.

—Joe Mullane, Redwood City, Calif.

Removing Labels

ANYONE WHO HAS SCRUBBED FRUITLESSLY on the gum labels and glued-on instructions that decorate plumbing fixtures will appreciate a can of WD-40. Used with a soft cloth, the lubricant works well as a solvent to lift labels off ceramic fixtures without a scratch. It works equally as well on metal.

—Duane L. Schubauer, Blackhawk, S.D.

Clean Cuts for Recessed Cans

ELECTRICIAN MEL MINOR installs a lot of recessed light fixtures in ceilings. In some cases he has to cut the hole in the drywall as well as mount the fixture in the ceiling joists. To keep the mess to a minimum, he makes the circular cutouts with the clever contraption in the drawing at right.

Although it looks like a harpoon, this tool is actually a jumbo hole saw affixed to a pipe extension. Mel made the rig out of sections of ½-in. galvanized pipe, joined with couplings, and a threaded shaft at one end that fits into the chuck of his ½-in. drill.

Beneath his hand is a hefty section from a plastic 5-gal. water bottle. The water bottle is glued to a sleeve made of PVC pipe. So when the shaft turns, the bottle remains stationary as it catches the dust.

—Gary M. Katz, Reseda, Calif.

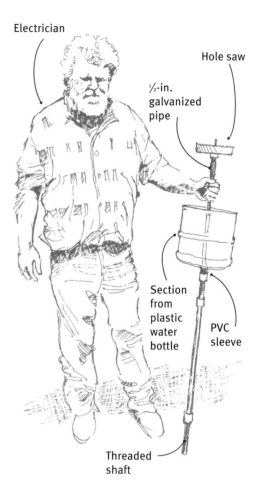

Electrician

Hole saw

½-in. galvanized pipe

Section from plastic water bottle

PVC sleeve

Threaded shaft

New Soldering in Old Plumbing

ONE OF THE PROBLEMS I have when remodeling an old kitchen or bathroom occurs when I have to sweat-solder new fittings into an existing copper water-supply line. It is almost impossible to get all of the water out of the pipes, and that leads to poor solder joints.

My solution is to drain the pipes in the usual manner—being sure to open faucets at the highest point in the system—and then use my wet-vac to suck the remaining water out of the lines. This procedure requires a vacuum-nozzle reducer to ensure a tight fit and good suction (I use the plastic reducer that connects my orbital sander to its dust bag). Remember to vacuum both the uphill and downhill ends of the line. I find that after about two minutes the pipes are dry and ready to solder.

—Peter D. Ellis, Needham, Mass.

Site-Built Wire Spinner

WORKMANLIKE WIRING is easier to achieve with a wire spinner. The site-built version shown in the drawing at right was whipped up by electrician Phil Clements in about 15 minutes, using a handful of wire staples, a few 16d nails, a fender washer, assorted 2x4 offcuts, and some short lengths of nonmetallic sheathed electrical cable (Romex). Phil first nailed together a pair of 2x4s to make a post about 24 in. tall, and then attached the 24-in.-long base pieces. He next stapled the short lengths of wire cable to create a loose cradle that holds a coil of wire as it comes from the box. Hung from a nail in a ceiling joist or door header, Phil's wire spinner rotates on the washer as he pulls and uncoils flat lengths of wire without twists or kinks.

—M. Scott Watkins, Arlington, Va.

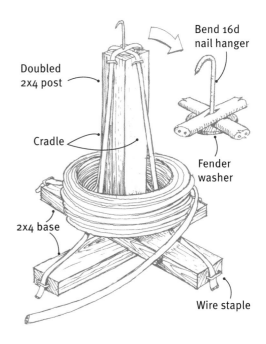

Bend 16d nail hanger

Doubled 2x4 post

Cradle

Fender washer

2x4 base

Wire staple

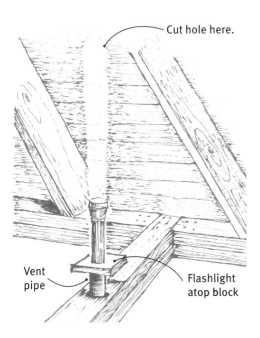

Cut hole here.

Vent pipe

Flashlight atop block

The Flashbob

AS A PLUMBER, I have to cut plenty of holes in roofs for vent pipes. One way to locate the spot for the hole is to hold a plumb bob over the vent pipe stub and then mark the vent's centerline on the roof sheathing. But this can be cumbersome in a tight spot. I've found that a better way to locate my vent cuts is with a narrow-beam flashlight. As shown in the drawing at left, I place the flashlight atop a wood block over the vent stub. If I'm concerned about the flashlight shining straight up, I check it for plumb with a torpedo level. Held plumb, the light shows the way to my target.

—F. X. Lowry, Somerville, Mass.

Toilet Transportation

PULLING THE TOILET IS A NECESSARY EVIL when replacing the bathroom floor covering. Here are a couple of tricks that make the job a little easier.

After shutting off the water and emptying the tank with a final flush, I rapidly pour two or three gallons of water into the bowl. This creates a siphon action that leaves the bowl almost empty. Then I set the toilet in a shallow wooden box with inside dimensions approximately 12 in. by 16 in. The box is mounted on casters, as shown in the drawing at right. Now I can roll the toilet out of harm's way without dribbles or back strain. By the way, some newspaper in the bottom of the box will help soak up moisture.

—Gary Goldsberry, Stillwater, Okla.

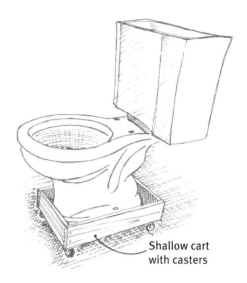

Shallow cart with casters

Flux-Brush Container

AS ALL GOOD PLUMBERS KNOW, one of the secrets of a successfully sweated joint is cleanliness. And one of the hardest things to keep clean is a flux brush. If you keep it in a toolbox, it just collects dirt.

I keep my brushes clean in storage tubes made of ¾-in. PVC pipe. For each brush, I cut a piece about 7 in. long and close its ends with a couple of PVC caps. Now my brushes stay clean, and the white containers make them easy to find.

—Alan Mendelsohn, Indianapolis, Ind.

Nonstick Cap for PVC Cement

WHEN I AM USING PVC CEMENT, the cap inevitably sticks to the container no matter how carefully I try to keep the cement off the outside of the threads and the inside of the cap. To prevent the problem, I just smear a little bit of petroleum jelly on the threads. Now no more glued-shut glue pots for me.

—Gary Easton, Roff, Okla.

Cutting Plastic Pipe

WHILE ON ONE OF MY DAILY INSPECTION TOURS of the job site, I saw out of the corner of my eye my plumber doing what looked like an aerobic exercise while standing shoulder deep in a narrow ditch. With sweat running down his face, he was rapidly pulling back and forth on a piece of nylon mason's line. When I asked him what he was doing, he gave me one of those you-ignorant-dweeb looks and replied that he was cutting a piece of 4-in. ABS plastic drain pipe. Sure enough, he had just made a perfectly straight cut through the piece of pipe. The pipe was almost totally buried in the narrow ditch, in a position that would have been tough to reach with even a reciprocal saw.

The plumber had threaded the line under the pipe, as shown in the drawing at right. Then he used a quick sawing motion to cut—maybe burn is a better term—the pipe in half. The trick to doing it right is to use enough line so that you can make long passes, pumping back and forth, or up and down as the case may be. Don't stop, or the line will seize in the melted kerf.

It turns out that mason's line will cut ABS and PVC pipe, in both schedule 40 or 80. The method is equally useful for flush-cutting a pipe where it emerges from a wall or a slab.

—Craig Savage, Carpenteria, Calif.

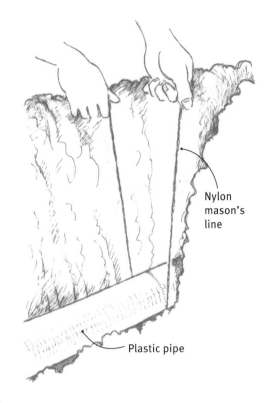

Nylon mason's line

Plastic pipe

Electrician's Stick

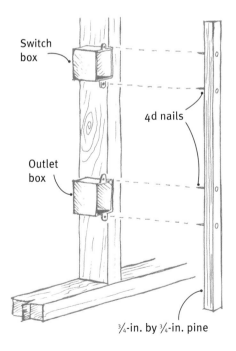

Switch box

4d nails

Outlet box

¾-in. by ¾-in. pine

THE NEXT TIME YOU HAVE TO affix electrical boxes to stud framing for switches or outlets, try using the jig shown in the drawing at left to position the boxes. I make the jig out of a strip of ¾-in. by ¾-in. pine. Two pairs of 4d nails driven through the stick correspond to the threaded holes in the boxes. To use the stick, position the boxes over the nails and place the stick on the floor adjacent to the stud. Now you can nail the box to the stud, and the height will be right every time.

—Santo A. Inserra, Jamestown, N.Y.

Unrolling Electric Cable

IF YOU'VE EVER PULLED ELECTRIC CABLE OUT OF ITS COIL in a random manner, you know how the wire loops can get curlier than Shirley Temple's hair. There is a better way. I make a simple plywood spool, as shown in the drawing at right, a little larger in diameter than the coil—about 14 in. I sand the edges of the plywood to avoid cuts and splinters, and I drill it for a length of sturdy dowel. A spacer, such as the one shown here made of 1x stock, goes between the disks. Plywood blocks screwed from opposite sides to the axle unite the spool.

To use it, hang the dowel from adjacent studs or tack the wire to the floor and roll the spool across the floor with a good shove. Either way, the wire will be nice and straight.

—Michael A. Meredith, Springfield, Va.

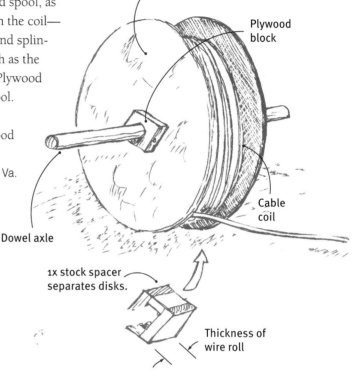

14-in.-dia., ½-in. plywood disks

Plywood block

Cable coil

Dowel axle

1x stock spacer separates disks.

Thickness of wire roll

Fishtape Target

IN ORDER TO SAVE ourselves some expensive plaster repairs, my partner and I decided to route our new electrical wires directly from the basement to the attic. We bored holes into the same stud cavity from above and below, but we had a terrible time trying to fish the new wire past the joist and the wall plates over the basement.

Then we hit upon the idea of dropping from the attic into the stud bay a plastic bread bag tied to a string. Once the bag was at the bottom of the cavity, it made a big, easy-to-snag target that was quickly caught with our fishtape and pulled into the basement.

—David Gelderloos, Boulder, Colo.

Ground-Rod Driver

DRIVING A GROUND ROD FOR AN ELECTRICAL SYSTEM can be a tedious task if you don't have the right equipment. The problem is putting the force of the mallet where you want it. The end of a ground rod is a pretty small target.

The drawing at right shows a homemade ground-rod driver that can help you deliver accurate force to the rod with each blow. One end of the driver is a 3-ft. length of ¾-in. pipe. The other end is a 1-ft. length of the same material. The two ends are linked by a pair of couplings with a short length of threaded rod. Be sure the pipe and the rod are screwed into the coupling as far as possible.

Start driving by slipping the 3-ft. length of pipe over the rod. The bottom of the threaded rod striking the top of the ground rod drives it deeper, and with the end of the rod thus contained, you can deliver maximum force to the rod without worrying about the business end of the driver—the section of threaded rod—slipping off the target. If necessary, you can add weight to the rig at the threaded joint. Use the short end of the driver to finish the installation.

—Don E. Schaufelberger, Phoenix, Ariz.

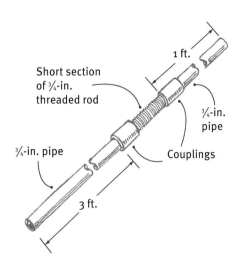

1 ft.

Short section of ¾-in. threaded rod

¾-in. pipe

Couplings

¾-in. pipe

3 ft.

Clamp-Nailing

SOMETIMES AN ELECTRIC OUTLET OR SWITCH BOX has to go between a couple of studs that are so close together, there's no room for a hammer or a drill bit. In this case, I reach for a C-clamp. As shown in the drawing at left, a clamp can be used to squeeze a nail into the stud. For good bearing, I use roofing nails during this operation. Occasionally, I find it's necessary to drill holes in the side of the box for the nails.

—Dave Kohler, Clarks Summit, Pa.

Pull nail into stud when space is too tight to swing a hammer.

The Cobra Light

As an electrician, I spend time in crawl spaces running wires. For a quick trip, a flashlight is more convenient than a drop light—especially when space is tight. As shown in the drawing at right, I use a sheathed electrical cable offcut to wrap my flashlight into a standup fixture. This gives me another hand when I need it.

—Janet Scoll, Richmond, Calif.

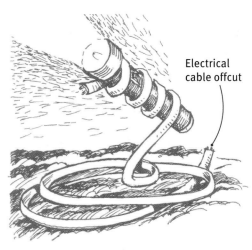

Electrical cable offcut

Balloon Plug

I had to glue a threaded fitting onto a piece of plastic pipe that kept dribbling water onto the bonding surfaces. To slow the flow, I got out the bike pump and an ordinary balloon. As shown in the drawing at right, I slipped the balloon over the end of the air hose and ran the hose through the fitting and into the pipe. Inflated, the balloon stopped the dribble long enough for me to dry off the parts and glue them together.

—Ed Self, Los Gatos, Calif.

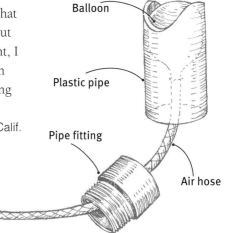

Balloon

Plastic pipe

Pipe fitting

Air hose